ALSO BY MIKE MICHALOWICZ

The Toilet Paper Entrepreneur

The Pumpkin Plan

Profit First

Surge

Clockwork

Fix This Next

GET DiffERENT

MARKETING
THAT CAN'T BE IGNORED!

MIKE MICHALOWICZ

PORTFOLIO / PENGUIN

Portfolio / Penguin
An imprint of Penguin Random House LLC
penguinrandomhouse.com

Most Portfolio books are available at a discount when purchased in
quantity for sales promotions or corporate use. Special editions, which
include personalized covers, excerpts, and corporate imprints, can be created
when purchased in large quantities. For more information, please call (212)
572-2232 or e-mail specialmarkets@penguinrandomhouse.com. Your local
bookstore can also assist with discounted bulk purchases using the Penguin
Random House corporate Business-to-Business program. For assistance in
locating a participating retailer, e-mail B2B@penguinrandomhouse.com.

Library of Congress Cataloging-in-Publication Data
Names: Michalowicz, Mike, author.
Title: Get Different: marketing that can't be ignored
Mike Michalowicz.
Description: New York: Portfolio, 2021. | Includes index.
Identifiers: LCCN 2021007922 (print) | LCCN 2021007923 (ebook) |
ISBN 9780593330630 (hardcover) | ISBN 9780593330647 (ebook)
Subjects: LCSH: Marketing—Planning. | Branding (Marketing)
Classification: LCC HF5415 .M5273 2021 (print) |
LCC HF5415 (ebook) | DDC 658.8—dc23
LC record available at https://lccn.loc.gov/2021007922
LC ebook record available at https://lccn.loc.gov/2021007923

Printed in the United States of America
1 3 5 7 9 10 8 6 4 2

Book design by Alexis Farabaugh

This book is dedicated to you, my reader.

*Go to **immersewithmike.com** and experience
this book with me as you read it.*

Let's do this together!

⟨ Contents ⟩

Introduction

Yeah, no.

Introduction schmintroduction. Let's cut to the chase. You and I have a crucial job to do—as in the life or death of your business kind of crucial.

You offer something people need, something a lot of people will love. Or at least something a lot of people *would* love, if only they knew about it.

What good is your offer if no one knows it exists?

The lack of marketing—good, effective, *different* marketing—is the driving reason for small business mediocrity and stunted growth. Too many great products and services languish in obscurity. We will not stand for that. By the end of this book, we are going to make sure you get noticed and get results in a crowded market—no matter what.

Are you ready?

Let's market the shit out of your business!

~~~~~~~~~~~~~~~~~~~~

CHAPTER ONE

Your Responsibility to Market

did inhale.

Yanik Silver blew a cloud of pot smoke right into my face. I had only one option: breathe it in.

I never anticipated that my greatest lesson in marketing would come during a game of billiards, capped with a ganja exclamation mark. It was the contact high that lasted a lifetime.

Yanik is considered by many to be the godfather of internet marketing. He helped innovate the use of email marketing in the early days, when people still looked forward to hearing AOL's iconic notification "You've got mail." Back when people thought an innovative website was one with an animated "under construction" GIF, he pioneered long copy sales pages with professional product images and clear call-to-action buttons. Yanik's marketing savvy yielded the company of his dreams, Maverick1000. He created a global network as a manifestation of his life's purpose: to help support visionary entrepreneurs grow their businesses and have a bigger impact on the world.

I had just launched my first book, *The Toilet Paper Entrepreneur*, and I had bought into the belief that a "great book will sell itself," hook, line, and sinker. I believed it so much that I feared I'd run out of copies during the first month. After all, if you build it, they will come, right? So I scratched together money through friends, emptied my "break only in case of an extreme emergency" emergency savings account, and ordered twenty thousand hardcover copies—all of which were now sitting in a fulfillment center, gathering dust. My book launch flopped. On release day, I sold zero copies. Zippo. Nada. Zilch. Do you feel me? My own mother didn't buy a copy that day. Ouch.

Defeated, I had two choices: learn how to market effectively, *fast*, or abandon my dream.

But where to begin? The strategies touted by some successful marketers at the time nauseated me. Marketing online by 2005 had become so commonplace, people doing it had a title: infomarketers. At least to their faces they were called infomarketers. Behind their backs, the smarmy ones were called names I won't repeat here. You know the ones I'm talking about. Some guy stands in front of a private jet (that isn't his) on a tarmac (that he sneaked onto), leaning on a new Bentley (which he rented for a few hours), and promises you the world. Their methods were gross and inauthentic at best, manipulative and predatory at worst.

Yanik always played a bigger game beyond the tactic of the month, and he didn't need to "prove" he knew his stuff with disingenuous pictures and messaging. Yanik marketed authenti-cally, genuinely, real-ly, and *that* is why I sought out his advice.

I desperately wanted people to notice my book, but I didn't want to use those gross info-smarm-eter tactics. So instead I had tried to follow "book-marketing checklists" in the way all tradi-tional authors are told to market—send out a press release, throw a launch party, start a blog, get a big-name endorsement—and yet all my efforts failed to generate anything beyond onesie-twosie book sales.

Twisting my cue stick, I shared my frustrations with my new confidant.

"Five ball. Corner pocket."

Moving through the table with ease, Yanik called out shots, and the balls rolled into the pockets at his every command, all the while listening intently to my story. He capped the game by sinking the eight so expertly that the cue ball slowly rolled back to the exact spot for the start of the next game. Meanwhile, I stood off to the side like a potted plant. A potted plant that over-shares its story of struggle, but a potted plant, nonetheless.

The game finished, Yanik motioned for me to grab my beer and head outside to the deck with him to look out over the roll-ing hills of Maryland. After what felt like one of those too-long, dramatic crescendo movie moments, he asked, "Is your book better than the stuff everyone else offers?"

"Yes."

"Does your book serve the reader better than those infomar-keters?"

"Hell yes. It is everything I know. It will serve entrepreneurs."

"If customers buy the infomarketer stuff and don't buy yours, what will happen?"

"They will be swindled, Yanik. My book is better than all that crap. I really believe that to my core."

Yanik smiled, as though I had finally given him the answer he wanted. "Then you have a *goddamn* responsibility to outmarket them."

Whoa.

On the little table next to him, Yanik started rolling a joint. "If people are buying shit," he continued, "it may be *their* problem, but it's *your* fault."

Despite the warm weather, chills ran down my spine. He was right. It *was* my responsibility, and if I felt I had a viable alternative to the crappy business advice out there, it was my own damn fault if people didn't know about it.

Yanik let me sit with the truth bomb he just dropped as he finished rolling his joint. Then he said, "People will buy, that is not the question. But they can only ever buy what they are aware exists. If your solution is better, you have to *make* them notice."

Then he took a hit off the joint and inadvertently blew the smoke right into my face. It was a profound moment. I breathed it all in, including the ganja cloud.

Yanik leaned back in his chair and contemplated the horizon. "Mike, what's your greater why?"

"My *greater* why? What do you mean?"

"Why are you here on this planet? What impact are you meant to have on our world?"

Damn, bro. I just wanted to sell some books, and sensei Yanik wanted to talk about the meaning of life. Then again, who am I to question a marketing savant?

Maybe a superior force intervened. Maybe in my heart I had always known the answer. Or maybe it was just the weed. But then I uttered the words that I have used ever since to define my life's purpose. The words that get me out of bed each morning and drive the long, hard days. The words that jack me up before every speech I deliver. The words that guided me as I feverishly wrote this book for you.

"I'm here to eradicate entrepreneurial poverty," I told Yanik. "That's my greater why."

"Entrepreneurial poverty," Yanik said, as if testing the words on his tongue.

I shifted to the edge of my chair. "Yes. I believe entrepreneurs change the world. They are innovators and problem solvers. They can fix some of our biggest issues. And yet, most of them are just getting by. If I could help business owners get out of entrepreneurial poverty, they would be free to do those big things, the big things the world is starving for."

Yanik took another hit off the joint and said, "Then that's all that matters. If your books will help you achieve your greater why *and* they serve entrepreneurs best, you *must* find a way to market them better than anyone else."

My call to arms began with a contact high. Yours happens right now.

Your mission to market isn't about you alone. It is about something much, much bigger. It is about you, your family, your community, *our* world. If you offer something that serves, you must make everyone aware. We need you, but we don't know you exist. And that "not knowing you exist" part is your responsibility to fix. Starting immediately.

Quick, name something you do better than the competition. Are your services more thorough? Do you provide a better customer experience? Are you more available to your clients? Does your product last longer? Does your stuff make your client feel better than the competitor's? Do you understand the client's needs better? Maybe there are multiple areas where you are the winner. I suspect you were able to identify at least one "better" pretty darn fast. Probably multiple. So, it is likely verifiably true. You are better.

And if your offer is better than the alternatives, in any single way, you shouldn't *try* to market to your prospect, you *must* market to them. You have a responsibility to beat competitors, big and small companies alike—the unscrupulous companies, the companies who give less, and the companies who care less than you do about the people you serve. Otherwise, you are letting your customers get ripped off. You have a responsibility to treat your customers and prospects right by marketing the hell out of your company. If you have a better option for your clients and prospects, yet they don't know it exists, they are forced to settle. That may be *their* problem, but it is *your* responsibility to fix it.

Great Offers Need Different Marketing

That day at Yanik's house, he reminded me of my life's purpose: to eradicate entrepreneurial poverty. Far too many business owners were (and still are) building businesses to gain financial freedom and control over their lives, yet were (and still are) in a constant cash crisis and feel exhausted. Fixing that gap between the dream of freedom and the reality of struggle was (and still is) my life's purpose. That's why I wrote my first book, this book, and every book in between. *The Toilet Paper Entrepreneur* wasn't a "better business card." It wasn't for "lead gen." It wasn't to make myself rich. I wanted to help my readers make real, lasting change. And yet somehow I had lost my way.

Looking back, I am still pissed at myself. I knew better. Building my first two businesses taught me that the *only* way to get in front of the people who need you is to master marketing, and that has nothing to do with mastering a marketing plan. Any plan is just fiction if you can't get prospects' attention in the first place.

The simple truth is marketing happens in milliseconds, not months. According to *Time* magazine, the average website holds visitors' attention for a mere fifteen seconds. Instagram reports people spend less than ten seconds on a post. And what about more tactile marketing? I'll bet you riffle through your junk mail at warp speed.

According to the Interactive Advertising Bureau, an ad must have viewer attention for at least a second for it to have any chance of success. If a prospect moves on from your marketing in less than one second, in the milliseconds, you've lost them. While a marketing plan is a wonderful tool to schedule what you know works, your number one priority is to first figure out what *does* work in those millisecond moments.

Try this. Right now, blink as fast as you can. That blink you just did, that took longer than a tenth of a second. The average blink is—get this—two hundred and fifty milliseconds.[1] According to

The Christian Science Monitor, thoughts can be spawned and acted upon in less than one hundred and fifty milliseconds. In other words, it takes longer to blink than it does to cognitively notice something *and* consider what to do with it. The takeaway? Successful marketing happens in a mere blink. Your prospect blinks and moves on or, if you do it right, stays. You need to win the blink.

The key to successfully marketing in milliseconds is simple: Be different so that people *must* take notice. Be different enough that the hardwired part of the human brain forces the prospect to contemplate and consider what they are seeing.

The irony was that while I had used out-of-the-box marketing ideas to beat the competition and grow my businesses to millions in revenue, when it came to marketing my book, I had fallen in line with the status quo. I did the *exact* thing that guarantees invisibility: I marketed like everyone else in my industry.

It took me a few weeks to realize why I followed the industry standard: I didn't consider myself to be "a real author." I wrote a book, yes. But I was just a newbie, and though I had confidence in my work, I didn't have confidence in what others might think of it.

It felt like the first day of high school, and I was the new kid from out of town. I was fraught with insecurity. Would I find my clique? Would they find me? Would I be welcomed? Or would the bullies give me an atomic wedgie? Just like the first day at a new school, launching a book, indeed making any meaningful stance, is a tenuous moment.

The truth is, I wanted to get noticed without being noticed. I wanted to reap the rewards of attention without the risk of getting attention. What if people thought I was too out there, too goofy, too Jersey? I had settled for the dull comfort of being unnoticeable rather than taking the soul-shaking risk of being unignorable.

It finally clicked. Sitting there on Yanik's deck, I realized that our own fear of standing out is the number one reason why we struggle to get noticed. People lose the game of marketing because they play by the rules—rules that don't even exist.

Once Yanik finally got my head right, I went back to the one strategy, the only strategy, that consistently works: market differently.

I thought about some of the infomarketers who were the real deal and didn't fall into the smarmy category. The common denominator? Ultimately, the good guys in the info space stood out by being different.

Jeff Walker, for example, marketed one and only one product, Product Launch Formula (PLF), for more than a decade and counting. He became *the* industry authority by doing what the others didn't. With no staged mansions, Jeff created videos from his Colorado mountain home, the same one he has had for twenty-plus years. No rented Bentley. Instead, he continued to drive his very used 1997 Ford F-350 pickup truck, because he loves it. When the competition zigged with smarm, Jeff zagged with realness. Different is not doing more of what they do. Different is doing more of you.

In my heart, I knew my book served others better than the alternatives, but so what? Better doesn't matter until you get noticed. And you won't get noticed until you are different. Atomic wedgies be damned.

Listen: You have something great. It's made of your imagination, your sleepless nights, your sweat, and your determination. It's a big deal, this thing. It's *the* thing. You know people—the right people—will love this thing. They need this thing. The problem is, you built it, and despite what the movies promised, no one came. Maybe not even your mom. And few will ever come, until you get different.

Maybe you have already invested in marketing strategies the presumed experts told you "everyone" must do to compete. Maybe you bought into copywriting courses. Maybe you hired copywriters. Maybe you even sent those copywriters to the same courses you took. You did all that and more, and now all you have to show for it is a depleted bank account.

You can't afford to advertise like the big boys. And you shouldn't (just sayin'). But you've got to peddle your stuff somehow, right? So you buy cheap media ads, Amazon ads, Google ads, Facebook ads, an ad company to run all the ads on all the ad platforms. And the cycle continues. You take another course to learn how to use advertising more effectively. You try direct mail. YouTube tutorials. Holiday promotions. And when that still doesn't work, you indulge in desperate wishful thinking: "If only I could run a Super Bowl ad, everything would change."

Despite all your efforts and hopes, you just can't seem to land enough prospects to meet your goals. There you are, sitting on this great thing, wondering if you'll ever reach enough people who will love it, need it, and celebrate it—the people who will *buy it*. They lose out, and you lose all.

Sadly, this struggle is justified in many self-deprecating ways. "I just don't know how to market." "Maybe this thing isn't as great as I thought it was." "Maybe those other things are better." "Maybe this thing I created isn't even worth marketing." "Maybe it's a dud."

I call bullshit.

The problem is not your thing. I know it's not. You are here, after all. You are reading this book looking to market what you have. What you have is great. It is needed. The problem is not with *what* you offer. Nor is the problem a lack of trying. Hell, you're pouring your heart into your business, doing everything you can to spread the word. You are doing what you think works. And *that* is the problem.

I know that may seem confusing. What I mean is that you're doing the marketing that already works for everyone else, which is the surefire way for that marketing to *not* work for you. If you mirror your competition, you are doing the one thing that guarantees invisibility. You must overcome your fear of being judged, step outside the box, and get different.

Look, the main reason marketing fails is because it falls in line with what "works" in your industry. Business owners keep doing what other business owners do, and that means everyone is trying to outdo each other using the same methods, just better. But when everyone is using the same methods, nobody stands out. A better version of the same approach is still invisible. When your marketing is like your competitors' marketing, you lose in the millisecond. The prospect sees some version of something that was deemed unworthy of their attention in the past, now repeated by you. A blink and they move on.

Why do we gravitate toward the so-called tried-and-true marketing methods? At the heart of it is a fear of standing out. We want to look just as good as everyone else, so we act like everyone else. We don't want to look like we don't know what we're doing. We think these established businesses all do it this way, so it only makes sense to do it the same way. We equate survival with conformity.

The problem is, if we focus on fitting in, how will our prospects ever find us?

Imagine you are in a room with five hundred people wearing identical gray suits. One of these five hundred people is your soul mate. How easy is it to identify your perfect match in a sea of gray? Hard. Nearly impossible.

Now imagine there's someone wearing a red suit. That person caught your attention—in a millisecond. So instead of going one by one interviewing the five hundred other folks for the next eight hours, it's just easier to start with the red suit person—and heck, you may even convince yourself that they're the one for you simply because they stood out to you right away. This example is for a soul mate. A friggin' soul mate. And the idea of wading through a sea of gray suits for hours on end is still exhausting. So just imagine how little energy prospects will spend to seek you out in your gray suit of invisibility. What chance do you have of ever getting noticed, even if you are their soul mate?

Most businesses don't wear red when the dress code is gray. Instead they try to be a *better* gray option: a darker gray, or a lighter gray, or a grayer gray. Even if they actually *are* better, how would anyone know? They're all wearing the same color.

Trying to do the same marketing as everyone else, over and over again, just better, will make you super frustrated. It's no wonder so many businesses think marketing is a waste of time and money. Who would be good at riding that merry-go-round? No matter which seat you hop on, they are all just painted horses on poles, going around in circles—going nowhere.

Do whatever it takes to remember this for the rest of your life. Write it down, post it on your bathroom mirror, tattoo it on your ass cheek. For God's sake, just don't forget:

Better is not better. Different is better.

Different is where you stand out within an instant, within the marketing millisecond. Arriving in red when people expect gray. Driving an old Ford F-350 pickup when everyone else shows off their (rented) Bentley convertible. Different is where you are undeniably noticeable, when you show up outside the context of what people expect.

Since my marketing epiphany, I have given keynotes to hundreds of thousands of entrepreneurs. I use these events to share what I know, of course. But the hidden gem is that I also use it as an opportunity to point out the danger of the status quo. I do this through live surveys, and this one in particular is my favorite.

"Pair up and share your most effective way to bring in leads," I tell them.

After a couple of minutes, I get out my flip chart and markers. "Everyone hold up your hand. Keep it up until you hear your lead gen idea."

Like the final round of *Wheel of Fortune* when Pat Sajak grants the contestant five popular letters before they can add a few of their own in an attempt to solve the phrase, I jot down the "big three" gimmes on the board: "word of mouth," "client referral," and "website." About 95 percent of the hands go down. I ask people with their hands still up to shout out their unique approaches. "Content marketing" is a big one; when I add it, most of the remaining hands go down. People shout out a few more ideas, such as "paid ad" or "trade shows." By the sixth or seventh idea, we've exhausted them all.

A room full of hundreds, sometimes thousands of business-people, all competing with each other to some degree, and they have the same six ideas. The same six ways they try to outdo each other, the same "gray suits."

In that little demonstration, they make it clear that they are all marketing in the same way. They all answer the same questions using the same language, they all follow the same "best practice" marketing models and strategies, and yet somehow they still believe they are different from everyone else. Even *seeing* a sea of hands drop at "word of mouth" or "content" doesn't tip them off that they are all the same to the world of prospects. Because even though they all do identical marketing, they *feel* as if they are better at it, that they stand out.

Or, worse, they take pride in the fact that they get most of their leads from client referrals. They'll say, "We don't need to worry about marketing; word of mouth is our lead source." The wishy-washy word-of-mouth strategy is no strategy at all. It is putting your marketing efforts in the hands of your clients so they do it for you, at their whim.

Waiting for customers to refer you isn't marketing. Word of mouth is a wonderful, albeit haphazard, source of opportunity when it happens. The key words being "when it happens." If a large percentage of your new business comes through referrals and word of mouth, you aren't marketing. You are crossing your fingers that clients will market for you. You don't have control over your company's growth; your clients do. Word of mouth should be the icing, not the cake.

Marketing the same way as everyone else is white noise. The only way for you to control your lead flow—where you can throttle up leads or, if you want, throttle them down—is to market in a way that is different from your competition. Get different. That's the cake.

Max Durovic was bored. Like, really bored. As part of his job working for a California deli, he had to stand outside holding a sandwich board for hours on end. But what if he didn't just hold it? What if he spun it? Sure enough, a spinning deli sign was far more entertaining for him than standing still. So he spun it on his finger. And with that, Max stumbled into different marketing.

That summer, Max invented "sign spinning," which is basically doing acrobatic tricks with arrow-shaped signs to advertise businesses. He says it is "as much a performance art as it is outdoor advertising." Have you ever seen a sign spinner? It caught your attention, didn't it? You see signs all the freaking time. The sheer volume of signs makes them invisible. The human brain is efficient at ignoring the inconsequential. But with a little bit of magical *different dust*, and a flip, spin, and twist of a sign, now you're staring at something your mind would have otherwise ignored.

In 2002, Max founded AArrow Inc., which has grown to more than thirty offices in ten countries worldwide, booking thousands of sign spinners. They even have an annual competition in Las Vegas. Different, done right, goes big.

A prospect's first experience with you, their first impression *of you*, is your marketing. If it is the same as every other business in your industry, your prospect can only assume you are the same, that you are just another ignorable sign. Different is marketing in a way that *no one else in the room does*. It is uncommon, unexpected, and unignorable.

Market differently. So differently that your ideal customers can't help but notice you from the sea of "top six marketing" white noise techniques your competition uses.

This is your call to arms, damn it!

You *must* market differently, because the world *needs* to discover you. Listen, you've navigated this pretty crazy journey called life to get to this moment. You might be doing this as a solo entrepreneur carrying all the burden by yourself. Or maybe you are the "new kid" who sits "somewhere in the back" of the industry. No matter your situation, status quo, good-enough, unnoticeable marketing is the risk. Taking the "risk" of getting noticed is the new safe bet.

Are you ready? This is your moment, kiddo.

The Reason You Could Fail at This

The day I emptied the truckload of my books was one of the worst, most exhausting days of my life. Yanik Silver had convinced me that marketing my book was my responsibility, but I still had most of my twenty thousand copies of *The Toilet Paper*

Entrepreneur to contend with. The distribution center charged me a one-thousand-dollar monthly storage fee. Because they weren't selling, I couldn't justify or afford the expense. I had two options: recycle the books, the soft term for turning my book into pulp, or ship them all to my house to save the carrying costs. I chose option two.

One at a time, I carried the boxes off the truck and into the basement, the attic, under my bed (replacing our box spring), in my kids' rooms, in the garage, and in the trunk, back seat, and passenger seat of my car. Sweat dripped down my body. T-shirt soaked and knees numb, I ached in places that I didn't know existed. And yet it was as if each box made me stronger. "Angrier" is perhaps a better word. I wasn't angry at myself; I became angry at my competition. I had twenty thousand copies of a book that could serve twenty thousand lives. I saw it as hoarding my own books from people who needed them. That pissed me off.

At the end of the day, every box unloaded and the truck long gone, I sat on the front stoop of my house and committed to sell each and every damn copy of those books sitting in my house. Not because I needed to sell them; because my future readers needed to read them.

I kept doing different, experimenting with new marketing strategies that would get my ideal reader's attention. Even after I started to get noticed as an author, even after I secured my first traditional publishing book deal, I continued to focus on selling that book. And I did. I sold every single copy. And then sold one hundred thousand more.

I could have thrown in the towel that day and let the books

collect dust. I could have sent that truck to the dump. I could have played it safe and shifted my focus back to businesses I had run in the past. But I knew I had something my readers needed, and I had a responsibility to market the hell out of it.*

Ten years ago I made a vow. I will forever find ways to make every business owner on this planet aware of what I have, even if my competition is bigger or more established or has a boatload of money. Because I believe my offer is the best solution for my readers, I have a responsibility to make them aware. I will never again wait for anyone to find me; I will make them see me.

You must make a vow, too. A vow to serve the members of your community by making them take notice. But a pledge is not enough; you must get past the biggest barrier to effective marketing: fear.

If you give in to fear—of the unknown, of standing out, of being vulnerable—you will not pull this off. Giving in to fear is the ultimate dream killer. You know that, I'm sure. Still, it's important that you understand that this book will help you only if you take action. You have to make the choice, right now, to stick with this marketing system, despite your fear.

Do you want to be safe or successful? This is a profoundly serious question. Ponder this, please, before you answer. I'm guessing you will say "successful," but do you mean it? Do you really, really mean it? Sadly, most people don't.

Most people choose safety over success and demonstrate that

---

* If you want to know more about how I marketed my books, you can read about it in the June 2013 *Forbes* article written by Dorie Clark, "How Mike Michalowicz Went from Unknown Self-Published Author to Mainstream Publishing Success." You can access it, along with all of the free resources, on my website at gogetdifferent.com.

through their actions. They *say* they want to be daring and bold, but they are not willing to discard the security of their commonality cocoon. They are afraid to put themselves out there, to risk humiliation or ridicule. They don't want to spin the sign—not for fear of dropping it as much as the fear of being *seen* dropping it. If you aren't willing to break the rules—which, notably, aren't *the* rules, but are *your* rules—you will also be stuck in the safe-feeling land of the unnoticed.

Marketing is not a game of hide-and-seek. It is a mission to be as obvious and noticeable as a lighthouse. Don't hope to be found. Demand people see you. You're the beacon of the best choice in the fog of mediocrity. I'll say it again, because you can't hear it enough: you have a responsibility to outmarket your competition. Your journey may have you riding the bench at times, or a lot of the time, but unless you try and keep trying, you will simply be that "person with so much potential" who never gets discovered. Dare to step up and stand out. Dare to be different. The world depends on it.

Mission Meets Nemesis

On a hike with my daughter along the rim of the Grand Canyon, I looked out over the expansive chasm and wondered, What would motivate a person to get from one side to the other? A dream, yes. It would have to be a big dream. But would that be enough to stick with it, no matter what the ordeal? Maybe not. Many people have given up on their dreams before completing them.

But what if it were a mission? What if my daughter were on the other side of the canyon? What if her life depended on my crossing? Hiking down one side and up the other for a grueling twenty-plus-mile hike? And what if a villain were crossing the same canyon, with the intent of destroying her? Now it is not a dream; it is a mission. The life of a loved one is in imminent jeopardy. And the outcome is fully in my hands. If I make the extraordinary journey, she lives. If I fail, she perishes and so does my soul.

The clients you serve are in peril. The bad guy is going for them. You have something bigger than a dream here. You have a mission: save your clients. And you must get to them before the villain does, regardless of the challenges you will face and the chasm you must cross.

Without giving it much thought, answer this question: Who is your nemesis? Mine is a guy who is the picture-perfect example of the info-manipulators I loathed when I launched my first book, except he probably *does* now own the private jet in the background of his photos. He promotes bigger houses, more cars, and piles of gold as the definition of success. He defines winning not by serving his customers but by the failure of his competitors. Every time I see a pic of this guy, I cringe. He represents everything I despise about business-focused "thought leaders." The community his message speaks to and serves uses hundred-dollar bills to light cigars and spits on the "losers" who can't make enough money to do the same. The problem is, because he markets well, people will listen to him. And if they listen to him, greed wins, and honest business owners lose.

To keep me motivated, I have a picture of him in my office. Not just any picture—the most obnoxious of all his obnoxious promo shots. Looking at it reminds me that I am on a mission to eradicate entrepreneurial poverty through service. For the good guys to win, I must outmarket my nemesis.

It's not an ego thing. It's an old-as-time, us-versus-them thing. Coke versus Pepsi. Joe Frazier versus Muhammad Ali. Nerds versus jocks. And let me tell you, that can be just as motivating as—if not *more* motivating than—being of service. I can either throw in the towel or, with an enemy ready to destroy the exact people I am out to serve, say, "It's go time." Then nothing will stop me from crossing the chasm.

We all need a nemesis. It doesn't have to be a person; it could be another business, an ideology, or something harmful to your community. We all need someone or something to fight for (our mission) and someone or something to fight against (our nemesis). When we have both, we become a street fighter for our dreams.

Want to know the name of my nemesis? Well, I'm not going to tell you. I won't give him that power. You can try to trick me into telling you, lock me in a room, force me to watch hours of "lowlights" of Virginia Tech football history, even give me an atomic wedgie, I still won't tell. This is my battle, not yours. And as much as I can't stand what he stands for, I don't want to send any negativity his way. I simply commit to outmarket him. Relentlessly.

Your Turn

I have compiled a list of action items and considerations for you at the end of each chapter in this book. Each item builds on the next. Don't skip any. Becoming a Different Doer (a person who does Get Different marketing) starts with a mindset shift. That's why the first chapter is your rallying cry. You need to realize that your mission is bigger than your fear. I am not trying to void you of fear here; I am trying to give you courage as you build marketing grit. And to do that, you need to start taking action immediately.

Don't bullshit yourself with an "I'll get back to this in a little bit" comfortable lie. Do the end-of-chapter actions. In most cases they will take you less than fifteen minutes. Just fifteen minutes. For permanent change. Permanently better marketing. Don't delay. Do.

1. Answer each of the following questions:

    a) Why must you outmarket the competition?

    b) Why is it more important for you to take the risk of getting noticed?

    c) Are you willing to do whatever it takes to step up and stand out?

    d) What will happen to you, your business, and your clients if you don't?

2. Next, identify your nemesis. Who or what is hurting the community you are meant to serve? Is there an unscrupulous person or company that is winning prospects' attention? Is there a whole group of marketers selling crap to your clients? Is there an ideology that needs to be squashed once and for all? What do you stand for and who or what do you stand against? Nail down your nemesis.

3. Commit to your marketing mission. Doing different is scary, I get it, but allowing your mission to fail as your nemesis becomes victorious is way worse. Are you ready to commit to your responsibility to market, regardless of the fear it may evoke in you? I want to know! Email me with the subject line "I'm Doing Different!" (so I can easily find your message in my in-box) to mike@mikemichalowicz.com. Share your mission in your note, and mention why different will serve you and your community. And, if you feel compelled to share your nemesis, I promise not to tell.

4. Download the free resources at gogetdifferent.com. The tools there will help you deploy all the techniques you are about to learn.

~~~~~~~~~~~~~~~~~~~

CHAPTER TWO

The DAD Marketing Framework

G abriel Piña loves cigars. When he arrived at the four-
day retreat I facilitated in the Smoky Mountains, he
carried with him a backpack and a rolling suitcase.
The backpack was for his clothes; the suitcase was for his cigars.

You'd think a guy whose hobby is stogies would have a certain Rat Pack swagger, you know, like Dean Martin or Sammy
Davis Jr. But Gabe? He dragged that suitcase behind him like a
man at the end of his rope.

Gabe founded Piña Business Services in 2007 to provide accounting and bookkeeping services to local businesses. He marketed using the common methods in his industry: the corner
booth at the conferences, email to prospects, free "industry reports." Of everything he tried, he relied heavily on word-of-
mouth referrals to grow his company. Despite these efforts, he

struggled to get enough clients to make ends meet. Bills and debt piled up, and up, and up. After relocating to Wyoming from San Diego in 2014, he had to contend with the triple whammy of being virtually unknown in the area, relying on word-of-mouth for new leads, and a looming bankruptcy. To be unknown and unnoticeable is a deadly combo that kills many good businesses.

The few connections that dribbled in were from all types of businesses. And, because Gabe's marketing presence (or lack thereof) wasn't different from other accountants, hardly any of those leads panned out. Being ignorable was crushing Gabe. That's why Gabe decided to go all in on different. Hence the trip to the Volunteer State.

When he arrived in Knoxville for the retreat, he faced two choices: stay the same and finally close up shop or "roll the dice" by doing marketing in an all-new way. Gabe is a fighter, and he was all in on saving—and growing—his business. We quickly decided the best solution would be to niche his offering and focus on serving a community that allowed him to combine his passion with his expertise. When you market to one community consistently, you quickly find the different that works and the different that doesn't. It allows you to do rapid marketing experiments and find effective, different methods fast.

"I want to be the authority in the accounting space for cigar shops," he told me on day two. "But I'm not having any luck getting new clients."

Gabe is a sharp accountant with a stellar reputation, and he knows the cigar world. It shouldn't have been too difficult to attract shop owners, right? In theory yes. The problem was, he still relied on his clients' referrals. He was unknown *and* unnoticeable. To save his business, he would have to market to his community like it had never been marketed to before. Not through an onslaught of mailers. Not through a desperate "you need to hire me, pleeeeeeeze" campaign. Through high-yielding, different marketing.

At the retreat, I walked Gabe through the same framework I'm about to share with you in this chapter. He came up with a different idea, evaluated it, and then conducted a trial. Within two weeks he completed the testing, within one month he had active and consistent lead flow, and within *six* months he had added six figures of additional annual revenue. That was a big deal for his business health, and worth celebrating with a damn good cigar. In fact, the experiment worked so well that Gabe adopted it as one of his key ongoing marketing strategies. I'll give you the specifics of how he did it in a moment.

Just before I sat down to write his story, I scanned Gabe's social media to check in on him and saw his post about buying his first brand-new car with profit he earned from his business. Now he has that swagger—not because he's the "cool cat" cigar dude—because he has the confidence that comes when you know you have complete control over your growth. You know how to get new clients, and *you* decide how to throttle the leads. To achieve this, you first need to have the essential understanding of *why* this process worked for him and why it will work for *you*.

The Science behind Different

"Crunching leaves are ignored, but the unexpected is watched . . . closely," Mr. Fordyce, my sixth-grade science teacher said during our first class. He delivered these words as though he were addressing the nation: lab coat, headset microphone, and all (for a room of nineteen students). That began our study of the caveman mind.

The word "caveman" is a catchall phrase for the prehistoric Neanderthal, *Homo erectus*, and that gigantor football player dude you knew in high school. Cave people were nomadic and formed hunter-gatherer tribes. For the most part, the men hunted food and the women gathered food. Regardless of whether they were hunting or gathering, their brains had the same objective: to ignore the superfluous and laser focus on the different.

When out and about doing the hunting and gathering thing, if they heard a recurring sound, such as leaves crunching or twigs snapping beneath their feet, their brains filtered out that extraneous noise, while sounds of opportunity, like deer hooves pounding on the ground, immediately captured their focus. Other times, they heard a sound that was a known threat, like the rumble of a woolly mammoth stampede, and they dashed toward shelter even before conscious thought kicked in, their feet spinning and kicking up dust à la Fred Flintstone.

And sometimes they heard a sound they just couldn't identify—an unfamiliar sound that just didn't compute. Now their minds paid full attention. It went all tunnel vision on them, scrutinizing the unexpected. Because that sound could mean that they had found their dinner—or it could mean that they *were* dinner.

Back then, prioritizing the different sounds and evaluating unexpected things was a matter of life and death.

Fast-forward to modern times. While technology and society have advanced at lightning speed, our brains have advanced far more slowly. Our good ol' gray matter is still designed to survive at the most primal level. Your mind is extremely efficient at avoiding known dangers, grasping opportunities, and ignoring the inconsequential (which is almost everything). However, one thing trips up the noggin every single time: different. But before we dive into that, let's take a look at *why* we ignore.

Have you ever noticed how quickly you can get over things? How quickly things become more of the same blah, blah, blah? It's called habituation. For example, the very first time you got one of those "Hey Friend!" marketing emails, you probably paid attention. Who is this long-lost friend emailing me? I haven't heard from "friend" since who knows when. And the fact that my good old friend calls me Friend, as opposed to my actual name, is so cool of them. Oh, Friend, you are just too much!

The next "Hey Friend!" email ain't so exciting, and by the third one, we have realized that this is simply the newest internet-marketer craze. You're not a "Friend," you're a wallet. Now "Hey Friend" emails become irrelevant, simply more white noise. Enter habituation, the process of ignoring repetitive, meaningless triggers. Blink—delete.

The habituation process exists within the reticular formation of our brains. The reticular formation is a network that emanates from the brainstem and maintains overall consciousness. It is a net, both literally and figuratively. It's the first line of defense against the millions of stimuli around us at all times. Right now, you could look down at your hand and spend the rest of eternity examining it. What is skin made of? Who thought of the word "skin"? Gosh, hand skin is just amazing. And on and on and on. There are countless things, right in front of you, always vying for your attention. But your reticular formation is doing its primary job perfectly: ignoring practically everything.

Have you ever seen a baby fast asleep while a fire truck roars by, sirens blaring? I have. In New York City. Many babies are so used to the traffic sounds they sleep right through it. That's habituation. And when a newborn baby first sleeps through the night without making a peep, the silence will often wake up their mother, who races to the crib to check on her baby. Why? She's tuned in to the unfamiliar—the silence—and perceives it to be a potentially serious situation. Maybe the baby stopped breathing, for example. Typical is ignored. Atypical is analyzed. That's how the reticular formation rolls.

Think about your last flight. On the airplane, seat belts click into place; people open and shut overhead compartments. It's all background noise. We recognize those sounds and our brains know to ignore them. Heck, it can be hard not to doze off as the flight attendants do their safety demonstration.

However, when the dude three rows back starts wildly waving his hands and speaking in a booming voice, we all crane our necks to check out what's going on. We want to know: Is he a threat or free entertainment? Is he going to get the plane grounded or will he make us laugh? We watch what is unexpected—closely.

Have you ever seen the Virgin America safety demonstration? A few years back it created a music video that was so funny and wild, most people actually watched it. They ignored the flight attendant standing in the aisle, demonstrating how to buckle a seat belt, zeroing in on the video the first time it played. And likely the second time, too, just to make sure they didn't miss anything. By the third flight and viewing of the safety dance video—not the "Safety Dance" video, my fellow Gen Xers—habituation had set in. Still, Virgin had won attention, for a short period of time, by being different. Different is the most effective way to get attention, but the shelf life is short. Therefore, different is not a onetime event, it must become an ingrained practice.

When something is different, the reticular formation triggers a cascading effect in the brain to analyze the situation, and the first priority is threat analysis. If we are in harm's way, it is critical to get out of it. But once the different thing is identified as safe, then our brains look for opportunity. Will I benefit from this? If the assessment is no, then our brains add this different, "Hey Friend"–type thing to the category of the inconsequential—something to be ignored. Opportunity exists in that little window between different, when the brain pays absolute attention to it, and the qualification of threats or opportunities, before the brain chooses to ignore this different thing forevermore. In those few milliseconds, you make your millions. Or billions. Or gazillions. And if you fail to respect or cater to this different-opportunity moment in the brain, you will be stuck in mediocrity—and so will your wallet.

The DAD Marketing Framework

We're still cave people when it comes to mental processing. Our brains still filter out the familiar and only take notice when something is different. This is why it is vital that you stop marketing the same way everyone else in your industry does and start "getting different." The reticular formation, the net, captures the endless stream of irrelevant junk and dumps it. When you market to your prospects, you must do so in a way that passes through the net. Fail to do that and you go into the heap of the ignored.

We avoid the threats, grab the opportunities, and tune out the irrelevant—remember, it's all about *finding* dinner and not *being* dinner. To market effectively to our ideal customers, we need to make sure that we get noticed, and that our ideal customers view what we do to get noticed as an opportunity, not a threat. But our work doesn't end there. Getting noticed by the right people takes us only so far. We need them to take action. This is the foundation of the three-step DAD Marketing Framework.

Here's how the DAD breaks down:

	DIFFERENTIATE	ATTRACT	DIRECT
GOAL	Attention	Engagement	Compliance
METHOD	Present something uncommon, unknown, or unexpected.	Demonstrate, exhibit, or express opportunity or benefit.	Specify a reasonable action to get closer to or gain the opportunity/benefit.

The DAD Marketing Framework

1. **DIFFERENTIATE!** *Do different to get noticed . . .*
    You've already learned why different works. This
    first step in the framework is to identify a market-
    ing approach that stands out in a sea of sameness.
    What will make your prospect's caveman mind
    stop and pay attention? How can you engage them
    during the first milliseconds?

2. **ATTRACT!** *. . . in a way that attracts your ideal
    prospects . . .*
    Next, ensure that your approach will appeal to the
    people you want to serve, not turn them off. How
    will you establish your marketing as an opportunity
    they will consider instead of a threat they will avoid?

3. **DIRECT!** *. . . and directs them to act.*
    Finally, your strategy must compel your ideal pros-
    pects to take a specific action you desire. Does the
    prospect see the reward of doing what you ask as
    greater than the risk of taking that action? And
    will their compliance with your directive help you
    achieve your marketing goals?

To sum up the DAD: *Do different to get noticed in a way that
attracts your ideal prospects and directs them to act.* That's it.
That's the framework. It's simple, yet powerful. When you follow it, you will land new prospects. Every. Single. Time.

Like doing the "YMCA" dance, you must do DAD in the exact
sequence for it to make sense. If you missed the "YMCA" dance,

that means you either missed the eighties (good on you) or you've never been to a wedding, like, ever. Google is your friend. Look it up. The dance begins with a *Y* up in the air, followed by *M* to your head and so forth. DAD works the same way. You need to do it in order. *D* to the *A* to the other *D*. They are the marketing "dance" steps you must master.

Always Differentiate first. You *must* gain attention by marketing differently. Most people skip this step and just try to put their most attractive offer out there. But you can have the greatest, prettiest, bestest offer in the whole wide world, and it will flop if no one notices it. Once you Differentiate, you do the next choreographed move and make it attractive to the people you want to—you guessed it, compadre—Attract. And you wrap things up by telling them specifically what to do next through a directive. Three steps, in the same sequence, every time. D-A-D. Always.

Sometimes, you're sure that your idea will stop people in their tracks, but all you get is crickets. For example, for my last book, *Fix This Next*, I created a parody called *Drink This Next*. It had the same design as my book cover, although instead of the yellow color, it was purple, and we hollowed out the inside so it could fit a flask of bourbon. I *loved* this idea and was sure that it would create a lot of buzz. But when we set up a test website to gauge interest? Crickets. No one wanted it—except my mom, ironically. Sigh. I still love that idea, but it failed to garner any attention. Even though I felt it was different, the actions of the prospects proved it wasn't different enough for them to take notice, so it was off the table.

I've also come up empty with the second step: Attract. I had what I thought was a great idea to garner new applicants for an open position. In the classified ad, I requested an interview . . . at three a.m. The ad got noticed, but the type of people who showed up at that hour were *not* the right fit for our company. I had thought that I would attract go-getters, people willing to go above and beyond to get the "right" job. Instead, I ended up with people who just got kicked out of the bar, and one UPS delivery guy who was so tired that he fell asleep in the waiting room. Odd interview time equals different but not attractive. It's important to remember that we don't want to be different just to be different, or we risk turning away the right prospects.

Imagine you are a criminal defense attorney. (I know. Dream job.) To win trials you decide to do something different to engage the jury. You wear a clown costume to the trial, complete with the big floppy shoes, squirting daisy on your lapel, and that *whacka whacka* horn thing. Yes, that is different. It guarantees attention. But unless your trial is with the clown community, it isn't attractive. It might be attractive at a five-year-old's birthday party, though even that is questionable. But man, oh man, the moment you do the second loop in the courtroom on your minibike, the jury is squirming to get away from you. No matter the evidence, you have lost the case. Different garners attention. Attraction garners desire.

But the DAD is not complete without a clear, singular directive. Now that you have the prospect's attention and they are engaged, you need to tell them what the hell to do. When I was talking with Jeff Walker, he explained that marketing is every step you take to get the customer to the buying decision, and the sale is the final action on their decision to buy. So your clear, singular directive should get them to the next step.

Forgetting to include a specific call to action is one of the most common marketing mistakes I've seen, and, admittedly, have done—repeatedly. One of the most memorable—and the most expensive in terms of time and cost—was the One-Nut Guy video I created to promote my book *The Pumpkin Plan*. We cast a crusty old local actor, hired a film crew, and created a series of videos.* The first one generated more than one hundred thousand views, which was awesome. The only problem was, I didn't include a clear and specific call to action.

The videos were different enough to get noticed, my readers found them funny (an indicator of attractiveness) and resonated with the message, and yet to this day, I have no idea whether it actually generated any book sales or compelled anyone to sign up for my mailing list. I never heard of anyone buying the book because of it and, double shame on me, had nothing to track to see if it worked.

Along with being specific, the Direct step must be reasonable. Maybe my marketing win is to sell you a house, but, once I have your attention, I wouldn't immediately ask you to plop down a million bucks on the spot. It's way too much, way too soon. It is *unreasonable*. A reasonable Direct could be to attend an open house.

An excessive ask will cause prospects to walk (or run) away. Conversely, inadequate asks will slow down (or stop) any progress toward the outcome you want. Once I catch your attention with uniqueness and maintain it with relevance, the Direct step must be specific so you know what to do, and reasonable so you feel safe doing it and move efficiently toward your goal.

---

* You can still find my One-Nut Guy videos on YouTube. Just search for "one nut" and "Michalowicz." Yes, I get my own joke.

I'm no stranger to marketing fails. But I don't regret a single one, because I learned from all of them. Every time I failed, after kicking myself, I would ask, What in the process was wrong? Where did it go off the rails? In hindsight it is always obvious that it was inevitably a failure in one (or a mix) of these three simple steps of DAD.

But, alas, it took me years to "decode" the Differentiate, Attract, and Direct steps. I tested the framework on my own businesses, and those of colleagues, clients, and friends, and refined and simplified it until I knew for sure it would deliver consistent results. None of the steps ever worked on their own.

Different always gets noticed, but it can also send people running. Attracting always gets people interested, but without different, it doesn't get noticed. Different takes attracting to work, and vice versa, but in order to get results, you also need to give direction. I had marketing that got noticed and that people consumed— cue the one-nut video—but didn't get results. A Direct fail.

The best solutions always work with humans as they are, rather than trying to force them to change. The DAD system works because it fits with our natural wiring, the way our cave people brains filter, analyze, and act on information. Differentiate, Attract, Direct. That order, that simple, every time. The rest of this book shows you exactly *how* to use DAD with the different marketing system, but just simply *knowing* the three-step process will massively improve your marketing game.

From this point forward, I want you to use the DAD Marketing Framework to evaluate whatever marketing crosses your path. It can be your own marketing, or a TV commercial, junk mail, direct mail, an internet ad, a radio spot, email blasts, a billboard, product packaging, an elevator pitch, *anything*. Simply ask yourself, "Does DAD approve?"

Try it now. Look at any marketing piece that is around you. If you're reading this book in the rarefied space of nature, then you can use the cover. Book covers are packaging, and packaging is marketing. Whatever you are looking at right now, ask, "Does DAD approve?" Go through each of the three elements. Does it Differentiate? Does it Attract? Does it Direct? If you say yes to all three, it passes. If you say no to one or more of the three steps, then ask yourself how you would fix that step. It is that simple.

Now I want you to go find another piece of marketing and do the DAD test again. Did you do it? Great. Now I want you to go do it once more.

By the third DAD test, you will have it ingrained for life. You're welcome.

After Gabe Piña shared that his ideal prospect was a cigar shop owner, we completed the DAD Marketing Framework for him— in minutes. Sometimes, different is something you already do that your competition does *not* do, and you just need to amplify it. This was the case for Gabe. He'd made a practice of helping people for free, without asking for anything in return. His competition did not do work for free, beyond the complimentary consultative call, which was really just a glorified sales call. Gabe did this out of natural generosity, not for personal gain, but he had since noticed that many of the people who received that help eventually hired him. That was our starting point.

Then, we considered how he might provide free assistance on a larger scale to differentiate. Free content, perhaps? A digital download? A direct mail campaign, with helpful tips?

"I don't want to send a glorified brochure," he told me.

In our brainstorm, we talked about Gabe's favorite business book, one that detailed a philosophy and system that he used when working with his clients. He came up with the idea to send that book to ideal prospects.

We ran the idea through the DAD Marketing Framework, checking off the components. He had a different marketing approach that would help him get noticed. Check. That approach would attract—not repel—his ideal customers. Check. And it included a clear and specific ask. Check. DAD approved!

Gabe returned from the Smoky Mountains retreat ready to run a test. He sent ten books with a Post-it on the first page that read "I hope this book serves you as much as it has served me," along with his name and email.

Getting the gift of a book in the mail is unexpected and different, at least for Gabe's prospects, so he got attention. However, many people don't have time to read a book, so most of them shelved it and got on with their day. Gabe tweaked the experiment and tested again.

This time, Gabe added *five* sticky notes. He placed them on key pages with messages such as "This paragraph gets results! Hope it serves you" and "Don't skip this page!" He knew people may not read the book, but they would look at the sticky notes because (a) it was easy, and (b) humans are naturally curious. The final sticky note pointed to a summary of the concept of the book. On the note Gabe wrote, "This will make your business achieve your goals. Text me and I will walk you through this, gratis." He added his cell number at the end of the note.

Again, Gabe mailed a book to ten new, ideal prospects. This

time, he had nailed the DAD components. It was different (a book in the mail), prospects were attracted to it (the sticky notes saved the prospects time and built anticipation), and it had a direct call to action (text Gabe to get free help doing it right). Gabe knew that if he could wow the prospect with the free help, they would likely want to hire him for all the future help they needed.

This different marketing approach worked even better than planned. Not only did Gabe pick up a client, seven prospects thanked him publicly for the book and posted pictures of the signed page—not signed by the author, but by Gabe himself. Genius! They added their own messages: "Thanks for helping me improve my business," and "Gabe Piña is the man!" Not too shabby a result for a second test run of ten books.

The experiment a success, Gabe rolled it out. He now mails an average of five books a week, which lands him two or three clients a month. Sometimes, he gets a call from a prospect who didn't respond right away, saying something like, "Hey, I got the book you sent a few months back. Can we talk?" If he wants to speed things up, he'll send out more books. If he wants to slow things down, he mails fewer books. Gabe is in *control of his business growth.* You can be, too.

The effect on Gabe's bottom line has been nothing short of game changing. And it is all a result of following the Get Different system. The cherry on top? Many of the cigar store owners reciprocate by sending Gabe free cigars. Now his collection is growing faster than ever with gifts from prospects. Do you feel me? Gabe's marketing is getting him both clients *and* a continual stream of gifts. What marketing does that? Different does, baby!

Different Is Just a Series of Steps

I'm not going to sugarcoat this: You are up against a powerful force that could take you down before you finish the next chapter. That force is the pull toward sameness. You're human, so that means you are more comfortable doing what you've already done and what other people in your industry already do. We humans have a constant need to conform. As much as we want to get noticed, we are also terrified of doing something noticeable. *Fear is the number one obstacle to creating remarkable marketing.*

The only way to beat that gravitational pull toward sameness is to take action. You need to punch fear right in the nose. You must do it, regardless of your trepidations. And the best way to get yourself to take action, no matter what, is to break down the steps into itty-bitty "you won't quit-ty"–size steps.

Justin Wise is a marketing genius. I wouldn't put it past him that his last name came through Get Different Experiments; he's that much of a Different Doer himself. Wise has a long track record of helping his clients get results. This is why I entrusted him to lead our Get Different Coaching System. Some people need coaching so they won't reject their best ideas, and so they will be accountable to them. Justin and our team walk people through the Get Different system and help implement the experiments.* Here's how Justin explains the power of breaking down the steps required to implement your different marketing:

"What's the first thing doctors do after an organ transplant?

---

* Go to gogetdifferent.com and get the free resources to see how we can help you ensure that you are doing Get Different right.

They pump you with a ton of drugs so your body won't reject the organ. Your body views the organ as a foreign object and will try to kill it. That's what your immune system is supposed to do. The drugs trick your immune system into believing, 'Hey, this liver is my liver. This heart is my heart.' That's what breaking down the process does for you—it almost outwits you into *not* rejecting a worthy, different idea. Small steps are the antidote to rejection. And, in doing so, your business thrives with its new marketing."

When I asked Justin for an example I could share with you, he told me about Valerie Donohue, owner of ChatterBoss, a virtual assistant firm based in Brooklyn, New York. "Val called me and said, 'Hey, I want you guys to run my ads.' I told her, 'We can run your ads eventually, but ads are really expensive. I'd rather have you go into ad placement when you are already over client capacity.' People use ads for lead gen, and when that doesn't work as well as they'd hoped, they are often told to go bigger with ads the next time. Spending five grand a month, plus an agency fee is not the solution. It's better to use ads to augment lead gen, not create it."

In talking with Val, Justin learned that she had wanted to run ads because more than 70 percent of her business came through referrals from one strategic partner and she wanted to diversify her lead sources so she could grow.

When Justin introduced the DAD Marketing Framework to Val, a CEO with a seven-figure business, she was shocked that she'd never thought about "this stuff" before. In one coaching session, they came up with a different marketing idea she could easily try. Like Gabe Piña, Val had a long history of being generous with her clients, and she regularly sent gifts to them. What distinguishes Val's company from others in her industry is Val's hires are not just task oriented, they are problem solvers. Building both on her generosity and her company's unique positioning, she decided to send custom baseball hats to prospects with the words "Thinking Cap" emblazoned on the front panel and a request to contact Val for a free consultation. It was different from the typical pens and water bottles her competitors often sent. And it was a demonstration of how her virtual assistants (VAs) could do some of the thinking for the business owners they serve. If prospects hired her firm, they could take off the thinking cap and leave it to the VAs.

Within minutes, the fear took hold. "She looked like a deer in headlights," Justin explained. It was fun for her to come up with the (damn good) thinking cap idea, but as soon as Val started to think about actually *doing* it, she froze. She was overwhelmed by all the things she would have to do to pull it off. Or better said, she was overwhelmed by all the things she *didn't* know that she would need to know to pull it off. I call this "the crash"— when your enthusiasm and confidence nosedive. If you don't pull up on the yoke, your confidence plane crashes with a "this won't work" or "let's back-burner it for now" excuse. This is where great, different ideas go to die.

"These aren't hard things to do," Justin said. "But when people hear the word 'different,' it becomes this nebulous concept. They become overwhelmed with not knowing what needs to happen next. In actuality, it's just a series of steps. The same as anything else they do in business every day."

So, Justin helped Val to break down her thinking cap marketing idea into small, "non-rejectable organ"–size pieces. First, call the swag company and get a quote. Next, make a list of one hundred people you want to work with. Then, get their email and mailing addresses.

"I kept asking her, 'What happens after that?' until she had the whole plan in manageable steps, along with who on her team would do each step," Justin explained.

Val's first mailing of fifty hats brought immediate results. Clients and prospects sent her pics of themselves wearing them (there is that reciprocity thing again), and she landed two new clients, one who cut her a twelve-thousand-dollar check right out of the gate and the other processed an eight-thousand-dollar payment. Move through the fears, take immediate action, land two clients, collect twenty large? Not too shabby.

To push through that gravitational "sameness" force pulling you down, break your first different marketing experiment into simple, manageable steps. Then, share them with someone who will hold you accountable.

~~~~~

"Your book is great, but it doesn't apply to me. We are in an established industry. Your different strategy will require too much change and too much time. Good stuff, Mike, but all theory."

My old college fraternity buddy, Greg Eckler (his nickname, which I am sworn to never share, is Greg Elk-Terd. Oops) owns a real estate agency. He kindly offered to read an earlier draft of my book and share his critical feedback. I sent the book, and twelve days later my phone rang.

"What's up, My Cow Shits?" he said. Fraternity nicknames die hard.

"Hey, Terd," I replied.

That's when he said, "Your book is great, but it doesn't apply to me . . ."

You may not be surprised that this is the most common feedback I hear about *Get Different*. You may be feeling that way, too. That the implementation will be too hard. That doing different will take too long. That huge effort is required. And with that, you may "discard" the book into the category of "Oh yeah, I read it. Great book. Reeeeaallly great book." And do nothing. That would be a shame. Opportunity lost.

As much as I wanted to invoke the lifelong fraternity rule of forty-eight paddles by the brothers for insulting an elder—I'm eight months older than he is, after all—I did the brotherly thing of helping a brother out.

"Greg, *Get Different* is not about the big changes or big moves. It is about doing what no one else does, at the most micro level. Look at all the common, industry-standard stuff people do in your industry. Pick the easiest and lowest hanging fruit to stand out. Determine where the industry is all apples and insert an orange."

"Well, all real estate agents argue the same points. They all are professional. They all are thorough. They all are great. But honestly, we are better than them. I just get frustrated that our customers can't see it."

"Doooooood. Did you really read the book? Remember, better is not better. Better can't be seen. It is hidden behind the cloak of industry sameness. A better apple is indistinguishable when it is among other apples. You need people to notice you before they can really see you and see why you are better. You need to insert an orange. It is that simple." Then I added, "Let's find the different right now."

It took us less than two minutes to have the first idea.

I asked, "Tell me about the customer experience. Tell me what every real estate agent does to sell a house."

"A selling agent will list the house online, perhaps run it in a paper, and put up a for sale sign on the property."

"Hold on, wait, does everyone put up a FOR SALE sign? Does every house get one?"

"Yeah, it's standard practice," Greg said.

Big fat hint here: when something is standard practice in an industry, that is a massive opportunity to be different.

"Tell me how the signs are posted," I said.

"They are put on the home's property, nearest the road. The signs are usually a sandwich board type or are a posted sign."

"How often are the signs posted that way?"

"All the time. It's standard marketing practice," Greg said.

"What if the signs were different? What if it was a small windmill. One of the tall types that you see in a garden? And what if the sign was mounted to that?" I asked.

"I have never seen that. No one . . ."

Greg paused. Then I finished his sentence for him. "Yeah, Greg. No one does that."

An orange among apples.

When you, my reading friend, come up with an approach that inspires you to say, "No one does that," you have found a different idea. Greg had his first idea: a windmill house for FOR SALE signs.

Different is not some massive change. It rarely is. Small changes that are different win. Different is hardly ever outrageous, but it is always atypical. The key is to break through the white noise of sameness. In many cases it doesn't take much.

Greg is off to test now. Maybe the windmill thing will work. Maybe it won't. The point is, he's off to implement a simple change that, if it tests successfully, he can use as his company's new "standard practice," which is anything but standard marketing in the industry.

If anyone knows different works, it's the police. Think about it. They *have* to get your attention. Otherwise, how will you know you're being pulled over because you were so busy blasting "I Can't Drive 55" by Sammy Hagar that you didn't realize the speed limit had changed? (Not that I would know anything about that.)

Here's the interesting thing about those police sirens—they've changed. The lights on the cars have, too. Many precincts have done away with the old pattern of flashing red-and-blue lights and the iconic low-high-low-high wail of the sirens. Now we have randomized blinking lights and chirps, honks, and squeaks. You already know the reason why: our brains are wired to ignore the familiar and notice the unexpected (aka different).

Notice that the changes to sirens and lights aren't radical, so sometimes they still go unnoticed by some people. I know I've been guilty of it, distracted by a killer tune on the radio, or, you know, by my own brilliant thoughts. But throw in a few more new sounds, maybe some random chirps, and bingo! Now they have my attention. Now I'm having my "oh, shit" moment. Was I speeding? Is my brake light out? Will I get arrested for playing Sammy Hagar hits? 'Cause I should. (On a profoundly serious note, I'm a white guy, so the thoughts and fears that play through my mind in that situation are likely far different from those of a person of color. I can't even begin to comprehend what some people have experienced, from police brutality and the soul-quaking fear sirens and lights can evoke.)

You don't have to change everything. You don't have to wait for a genius idea. You don't have to do something wild or complicated or expensive. Your different could be *just different enough* to get noticed. A few new sounds. Random patterns. Chirp, chirp. Done deal.

You don't have to be fearless or a superhero to pull off a Get Different Experiment. You simply need a few ideas, a bit of gumption, and the courage to proceed despite your fears. In the next chapter, we'll go deep on ideation. Even if you think you don't have a creative bone in your body, you'll easily come up with something to test.

I promise: you've got this.

Your Turn

Before we move on, let's first find out how other people would describe your different. Being totally transparent here—I want you to see how friggin' awesome and valued you are by the people who know you. If you don't see how you and your company are unique, that will undermine the DAD Marketing Framework.

You know those fun house mirrors at carnivals that show you a distorted view of your body? Most of us don't see our true selves. We exaggerate flaws and downplay our strengths, which can make it challenging to come up with inspired ideas and even more challenging to take action on those ideas. Let's start to fix that.

Step 1: Identify twelve people who know you (or your company) well. Four of the people should be new relationships of less than one year. The next four should be people who have known you (or your company) for over one year and less than ten. And the last group of four people are people who have known you (or your company) for ten years or more. You don't need to be in active communication or relationships with these individuals. You do need to have a way to contact them.

Step 2: Send the following message to each of the twelve contacts you have listed above:

The author of the book I am reading gave me an assignment I need to complete immediately. I am required to pick someone who knows me well, so I would love your help! I need to know what you feel my "Difference Factor" is: something I do better or

*differently than anyone else. Your response doesn't
need to be long. A sentence will do. I will use your
insights to improve our business positioning. Thank
you so much!*

If you are trying to identify your company's uniqueness
instead of your own, change the text to say, "I am required to pick someone who knows my company well"
and "I need to know what you think makes our company
different from most others: something we do better or differently than anyone else."

Step 3: Review the responses you receive from the contacts
and identify the three most common observations made
about your Difference Factor. You need at least ten responses for this exercise to be effective. If you don't reach
that threshold, send more messages.

Step 4: With the top three Difference Factors identified in
step three, consider how these themes distinguish you and
your company.

CHAPTER THREE

The Target One Hundred

You should know right up front, we are not doing Get Different marketing based on a hunch. No, we are doing Get Different marketing based on science—brain science, mostly, but also *you* science. The "you" part is the evaluation and testing part, where *you* determine whether a marketing approach is worth trying and track its effectiveness. To follow the science, you'll need a decent sample size. If you corner a statistician in a bar—as one does—they'll tell you most of them agree that the minimum sample size to get a reliable result is one hundred.

Data scientist Dr. Piroska Bisits-Bullen speaks actively on making data-based decisions. In her article "How to Choose a Sample Size (for the Statistically Challenged)," Dr. Bisits-Bullen shares some basic guidelines to ensure the data you analyze gives you an indication of whether the experiment will work on a large scale.[1] She states that a good sample size is 10 percent of the entire target population, and that a sample size should never be below one hundred people or organizations. If your target market has five thousand prospects, then you'll need a minimum of one hundred prospects and a maximum of five hundred for an effective marketing test. To gain the greatest assurance of your marketing effectiveness, test five hundred. To keep costs down, do at least one hundred. But you want to keep within that range.

For most businesses, one hundred prospects are enough to start a different marketing experiment. It's enough to get a mini-campaign going—enough for you to start building the different marketing muscle. And if your experiment is different enough, in many cases, one hundred prospects will be enough of a sample to land that first client or two. This is true for service businesses, products businesses, and nearly every other type of business.

Note that you can work your way up to reaching one hundred prospects. Recall that Gabe, the cigar-loving accountant whom you met in the last chapter, sent out ten books that first week, then another ten the following week, and so on, until he reached his sample size. He did it this way because it was easier on his bank account to space it out.

Let's think about it. If you could target only one hundred prospects, who would they be? Who are the top one hundred ideal candidates you are salivating to have as customers? I need you to know, because we are about to win them over.

To be clear, I'm not suggesting you imagine the *type* of people who you want to work with. I'm asking you to make an *actual list*—the contact's name, the company name (if applicable), email address, physical address, all that jazz. And if you don't have a clue who they are, I can already tell you why your marketing doesn't get you the results you want. I'm not trying to be a dick here (well, maybe a lil' bit), but if you don't know who needs you, how can you market to them?

Fishing for great clients is like fishing for, well, fish. Before you choose a fishing spot, before you bait your line, you need to know which fish you are trying to catch. You can be going for marlin all day long, but if you are fishing with worms in your backyard pond, it ain't gonna happen. And if you are fishing for marlin in the backyard pond, not only is it not going to happen, you're gonna look pretty weird strapped into a swivel chair pulling in a guppy.

The key to successful marketing is knowing the Who, What, and Win. Repeat that list in your head until it is engrained. Who, What, and Win . . . Who, What, and Win. Got it? These three mission critical elements nail down the ideal prospect (the Who), your ideal offer (the What), and your ideal marketing outcome (the Win). Know these three elements, and you will be able to market more effectively than ever before. And it all starts with the Who—your ideal prospects.

The Who

Don't know who your Target One Hundred customers are? Here's how to find them fast. First, start with your existing customer base—assuming you have one. If you don't, no wor-ries, I will show you how to make this list from scratch.

Start by printing out your existing customer list sorted by most revenue to least revenue over the past two years. It's important to sort this way because customers demonstrate how much they value you by how much they spend. We want to clone customers who like us and spend a lot with us. And while your existing customers are not necessarily representative of others in their category, they are a shortcut to finding more like them.

Once you identify the customers who value you the most, do a crush/cringe analysis. Of the customers you have listed so far, whom do you love doing business with? These are the people who, when the caller ID pops up on your phone, get you totally pumped. You can't wait to hear from them and can't wait to serve them. Put a smiley face next to each crush you have on this customer list.

Now let's do this again for the cringers. These are those cus-tomers who, when the caller ID pops up, you say in your head—and sometimes accidentally say out loud—"Fuuuuuuuuuuuuggggg. Not these people. Not now." You will never make these custom-ers happy, no matter what you do. These are the folks who cause you to splash ~~water~~ vodka on your face and slap yourself on the cheeks before you call back. Those are the cringes. Put a frowny face next to them.

Now circle the top 10 percent of customers on your list who are the highest revenue (they like you best) and you labeled as a crush (you like best). You want more just like them. Think of a specific high-revenue client you love. Now imagine if ten of their clones walk into your office and plopped down some money to work with you. That would be a game changer for your business, right?

CUSTOMER	REVENUE	CRUSH/CRINGE
Hoolinium Co.	$50,000	☹
InterCommuTech	$35,000	☺
Umbrella Co.	$20,000	☺
North Integration Inc.	$12,000	☹
GlobalTech	$8,000	☹
Iscram	$5,000	☺
Fan City Tickets	$5,000	☺
Centralware	$5,000	☹
Amplex	$4,500	☹
Rangreen	$4,000	☺

The Crush/Cringe Analysis

With this simple piece of information, we can start building your list of top one hundred prospects. But what if you don't have any customers you want to clone? In that case, and it does happen, we clone you. What characteristics do you have that you want your customers to have? Knowing this information, we then look at the other people around you—your vendors, your friends, anyone in your circle—who are like you. Among these people, whom do you like the most? Those people can give you insights into the community you can target.*

At the end of the day, birds of a feather flock together. The shortcut to building your list of one hundred prospects is to start searching for their clones. Their competitors and vendors are likely like them. If Coke is your best customer, chances are their competitor Pepsi will be a great customer for you, too. If Ford the automobile manufacturer is your best customer, Goodyear, a manufacturer of tires and a vendor to Ford, is likely a good prospect opportunity to consider.

Here's the technique to nail down your group of elite prospects:

1. Write down everything you know that defines the avatar of your best customer, who brings in the highest revenue and you enjoy working for the most.

2. Start with demographics, such as industry, title, gender, age, family situation, and religious orientation. Then go deeper into their psychographic by defining their biggest problems and desired solutions. At the end of the day we are looking for great customers who have a big problem you are best situated to solve.

---

* I document the entire system to rapidly and organically grow your business in *The Pumpkin Plan*. What I just shared in this book are the basic principles. If you want to nail it, buy *The Pumpkin Plan* at your favorite book retailer.

3. Next, search for groups, platforms, meetups, conferences, and podcasts where your avatar goes to share knowledge, learn, be entertained, and, ideally, seek solutions for their biggest problem. That is where you need to go. You want to find these congregation points and market to them there.

4. Do a web search for "help for [avatar] with [problem]" or "help with [problem] for [avatar]," or a search for your avatar that specifies the problem. For example, if you own a nanny employment service, and you specify your ideal avatar is moms with multiple young kids, you might search "help for overwhelmed moms with twins." You will find websites, resources, meetups, and more. These are all places where your avatar gathers. See if you can get information on the participants, maybe partner with the site managers to share knowledge and connect with people; maybe you can purchase a list, maybe you can even offer to help build a list. Ask the hosts how to gain access to the people or propose how the host can win as you build your prospect list.

5. Do a web search that simply specifies your ideal avatar. For example, let's say you have a product that goes into planes and that your ideal customer is the established pilots who have a say on cockpit

changes. A search for "pilots who have worked for more than twenty years in the industry" or "how veteran pilots can influence what is installed in cockpits" comes up with many articles for organizations that talk about this community. These are people and organizations you can contact to learn more.

6. Social media platforms are a powerful way to build ideal customer lists. I am not saying that it is necessarily your primary marketing platform, but you can build great lists from these because they are so targeted. Give prospects something free in exchange for their contact info.

7. If you are in B2B, you can do web searches for the name of one ideal, existing customer and add the words "competitor of" or "alternatives to" in front of it. This is a great way to find potential new customers. For example, a search for "alternatives to Mike Michalowicz" caused the internet to collapse. I kid. It came back with a site called Goodreads and a list of a few dozen authors that "Goodreads members also like." One of them is 50 Cent, I presume because of my short-lived hip-hop career.* Or, more likely because he is an author of some

---

* When I say "short hip-hop career," it lasted as long as it takes to design a website—a few hours. If you want to see my fine work, do a web search for my stage name: Fat Daddy Fat Back, and you will be enraptured by different.

damn popular books that include lessons from his business career.

8. You can buy lists, too. Search for "prospect lists" and use the parameters of your ideal avatar to find them.

9. Look for your ideal prospects advertising (again ideal for B2B). If you sell services to computer repair companies, for example, search "computer repair companies near me" or "computer repair companies in [specify area]" and it will spit out a list.

10. For B2C do a search for "[avatar] clubs" or "[avatar] meetups" or "[avatar] support groups" or "[avatar] events."

11. Go old school and network. Blow the dust off your business cards and get out there. Go to the places where your ideal prospects gather, and get their business cards (or a way to contact them). The list builds in those meetings; the opportunities come about with the subsequent outreach.

Again, you are looking for what I call congregation points— places where these customers find each other. The goal is to insert yourself there. So, search in a way these customers would search for each other. What terms do they use to identify themselves? What is the problem they want to fix? Do those searches and see where they go. Then, find a way to gain access to the list. The gatekeeper in some cases will be the person hosting the site. In many cases, if you search multiple ways, you will find the information available freely.

Sometimes you will have to do more situational marketing. For example, as I am writing this, I am just starting the process of buying a new car. For a while, I wanted to have the latest and greatest. But now, I seem to be in some sort of weird reverse midlife crisis, because one day I woke up and realized I just didn't care so much. In fact, these days I get more joy out of seeing how long I can keep a car before it just doesn't make sense anymore. Like, right before I start keeping duct tape in my glove compartment so I can hold my car together. I'm not quite at that stage yet, but I'm getting there. So, how do you find me?

Well, a few ways. One is through web marketing for sure. People search for what's on their mind. I've conducted a lot of searches for cars, and if I looked at my search analytics, it would show that over time the frequency of my internet browsing increased and became more specific. So that is a behavioral indicator, and you can surely pay for advertising to attract prospects who conduct web searches relevant to your offer.

Alternatively, there are simply standard trends. You can search for "how often do people buy cars," and you will find a stat. Then you can use that stat to find congregation points. For example, if the average person buys a car every eight years, you can try to identify people who bought cars eight years ago.

The What

Now you know the Who to target. If you don't have a list of one hundred yet, that is okay. But you need something. Don't keep reading without doing. Gimme something. Anything. Even if you want to race along, give me ten names. You can do that right now.

The next question we need to answer now is "What?" What are you going to market to your Target One Hundred? I am sure you already had something in mind. I mean, you evaluated your existing customers, which means you are already selling something. And even if you based your prospects on you, you still likely had an offer in mind. What is it?

Knowing what you plan to sell, we now need to discover the reason these one-hundred-plus folks most want your offer. Yes, you do a million great things. I get that. But for them to notice you and be attracted to you, they need to know if you satisfy their core desire. Back to my car search. I have a main component in my decision. I want to haul stuff around. I like to do that; it makes me feel like a tough person. I like to cut up firewood and carry it home. I like building stuff; I'm planning a raised garden for my next home project. My version of a weekend warrior is me wearing work boots and being covered in dirt. It doesn't fit my self-image to do this in a small sedan, but it would work with a pickup truck. *That* fits my image. So, the big feature I want is a pickup truck, and the benefit is I feel more tough.

I also want an electric vehicle. I realize it may not make a huge impact on the environment, but it's a step in the right direction. Also, I don't like the smell of exhaust. I also want something that is small enough to park easily. I live in New Jersey, a state where people live on top of people, and when you do find a parking spot, it's a squeeze. I also want all the bells and whistles. Heated seats, power everything, and if it can give me a massage, too, I'm in.

The company that makes a tricked-out, electric-powered pickup truck that makes me feel like a toughy-tough dude and will last for ten years or more (with no need for duct tape) will get my attention. I'm getting what I want, and that's what serves me best, as a customer.

So ask yourself, what specifically is it about your offer that your ideal customers benefit from most? Before you can market to your Target One Hundred, you need to figure out the What that compels them most. The DAD Marketing Framework plays right into this. You Differentiate so the Whos notice. You Attract them by emphasizing the biggest benefit of your What. And you Direct them to act by having a clear Win.

The Win

The ultimate goal of all marketing is to achieve what you want. It could be to gain a customer or retain a customer. It could be to get a referral. It could be someone to volunteer time. Now that you know your ideal avatar (Who) and the thing you intend to sell them (What), you will identify the ultimate outcome you want (Win). This is the Who, What, and Win.

For example, let's say you have a roofing business. The Win

for you is a customer buying a new roof. The thing is, prospects don't necessarily have a list of roofers to call in their back pocket. More often their roof leaks and the homeowner searches their attic for the cause, hoping that someone left a bucket of water upstairs and a squirrel got in and knocked it over. But alas, the problem is a leaky roof, and their predicament is your opportunity to do some Get Different marketing. You need to nail the Who, What, and Win. The Who is the homeowner with the leaky roof. The What is a roof that doesn't leak. And your Win is the homeowner buying the new roof.

Remember that the DAD Marketing Framework ties into the Who, What, and Win. Once you have their attention and engagement, we need to Direct them toward the Win, with reasonable steps. Your Win may be getting them to plunk down twenty grand for a new roof. But if your marketing piece says, "Give us twenty grand now!" it may be too unreasonable an ask. Instead we need to move efficiently toward the Win, while being careful not to discourage the prospect from continuing.

So while the Win is selling a twenty-thousand-dollar roof, the prospect's first experience with our marketing would likely be to ask for contact information. Such as "Get Our Ten Must-Know Roof Tips" by giving us your email address. Or "get a Free Estimate" in exchange for their phone number.

Again, the ultimate goal of all marketing is to achieve what you want. Once you've determined your Win, then Direct the prospect to take specific, reasonable steps to lead them toward the Win.

The Get Different Experiment Sheet

You build confidence by doing, by taking one small risk at a time. In her book *The Progress Principle: Using Small Wins to Ignite Joy, Engagement, and Creativity at Work*, Harvard professor Teresa Amabile shows that regular, minor successes can be more effective than achieving a big success. She explains, "On days when people have made real progress in work that matters to them, they end the day feeling more intrinsically motivated—turned on by their interest in and enjoyment of the work."

To help you take these small risks, I've created the Get Different Experiment Sheet. You can download it for free at goget different.com. Or, if you prefer, you can simply use a piece of scratch paper or keep your experiments in your own journal. You'll complete components of the worksheet in this and the next three chapters. Then, in Chapter 7, I'll walk you through how to complete it from start to finish and determine whether your different marketing idea actually worked.

To bring clarity to our objective, start by filling in details for your Who, What, and Win. This will position us to do Get Different Experiments, so don't skip this step.

So you know you are not doing it alone, and so you have an example, I will do all the sheets along with you.

GD EXPERIMENT SHEET

FOR _____

DATE _____ TEST # _____

STEP 1: OBJECTIVE

WHO
Who is the ideal prospect?

_____

WHAT
What offer serves them best?

_____

WIN
What is the outcome you want?

STEP 2: INVESTMENT

CUSTOMER LTV: _____
The typical life-time value (revenue) of a customer.

CLOSE RATE ODDS: _____ OF EVERY _____
Your expected close rate of engaged prospects e.g. 1 of every 5.

INVESTMENT PER PROSPECT: _____
The dollar amount you are willing to risk to land a prospect.

NOTES:

STEP 3: EXPERIMENT

MEDIUM: _____
What marketing platform you will use? e.g. website, email, direct mail, billboard, etc.

IDEA:

DOES THIS COMPLY WITH THE DAD FRAMEWORK?

❑ **DIFFERENTIATE**
Is it unignorable?

❑ **ATTRACT**
Is it a safe opportunity?

❑ **DIRECT**
Is it a specific and reasonable ask?

STEP 4: MEASUREMENT

INTENTIONS	OUTCOMES
START DATE: _____	**END DATE:** _____
INTENDED # OF PROSPECTS: _____	**ACTUAL # OF PROSPECTS:** _____
INTENDED RETURN: _____	**ACTUAL RETURN:** _____
INTENDED INVESTMENT: _____	**ACTUAL INVESTMENT:** _____

OBSERVATIONS:

VERDICT {

EXPAND & TRACK	**RE-TEST**	**IMPROVE**	**ABANDON**
Use as ongoing strategy	Test new sample	Fix and retry	Start new experiment

The Get Different Experiment Sheet

STEP 1: OBJECTIVE	**WHO** Who is the ideal prospect?	
	WHAT What offer serves them best?	
	WIN What is the outcome you want?	

STEP 1: OBJECTIVE—The first stage of a Get Different Experiment, where the prospect, offer, and desired outcome are defined.

Here is what I came up with:

> Who: An "underdog" entrepreneur with a product or service that is superior to the alternatives, yet who is struggling to get noticed due to ineffective marketing.

> What: My book Get Different, which delivers a simple, powerful marketing framework that they will use forevermore.

> Win: They buy the Get Different book.

In my example, my Who is the ideal prospect. This is whom I specifically target with my Get Different marketing, but others may also be attracted to it. Maybe marketing personnel in a large organization would benefit from this book. Maybe a non-underdog entrepreneur will use it. The thing is, I market to a target community but I don't exclude others who may get caught up in the current.

When you look at my What, you will see my focus is on marketing this book. Sure, I have other things I offer, like the Get Different Coaching System and live events. But I need to narrow it down to the one thing that I am marketing. Do the same. Pick the one thing to market to the one community. One thing for one community per experiment. You can do countless subsequent marketing experiments to sell other things, as needed.

The Win is buying the book. Again, I'm focused on just one thing. I need to market in a way that gets my Who to buy the book. That's what this is all about. Once I achieve that outcome, I can introduce other Get Different marketing. Perhaps having a reader encourage others to read the book. But again, keep it simple: one action, for one type of prospect per experiment.

What Are You Willing to Invest?

Here is a critical question for you: What is the lifetime value (LTV) of landing your ideal customer, the revenue you expect them to generate for you over all transactions they do with you, over all the time they work with you? Alternatively, you can choose other calculations for LTV, such as profit or gross margin, but for simplicity's sake I suggest you base it on revenue and use a system like the one I outline in *Profit First* to ensure profit is baked into every transaction you have.

If you are struggling to guess your ideal customer's LTV, just look at the best customers you've had to date and multiply their average annual revenue by the total number of years you expect to continue serving them. I don't want you to get bogged down in the details, but I do need an approximate number. Does an ideal customer generate one hundred dollars of income over a lifetime? Or is it one thousand, twenty thousand, or seventy-five thousand? It is it more than one hundred thousand? Give me a rough number.

Now, let's look at the likelihood that you *will* land that customer. What are the odds—if you market directly and effectively to one of these ideal Target One Hundred prospects—that you will get their attention and win their business? These are Close Rate Odds. Before you answer, I want to know your best guess for the odds based upon your best marketing effort, if you put your best foot forward. One out of two? One out of five? One out of ten? If you aren't sure how to answer this, look at your conversion rates for past marketing efforts. Or look up average conversion rates for your industry.

Now, considering the LTV and your Close Rate Odds, what are you willing to invest per prospect to make that happen? Think of it like a bet. Maybe it's blackjack, or poker, or figuring out who will win at the Academy Awards. You figure out how much you want to put in based on the pool (LTV) and the odds of winning that pool (Close Rate Odds). How much would you bet? For real, how much? You know the winning purse. For the LTV of your ideal customer, how much do you feel is worth risking?

What did you choose? Did you bet ten dollars? Or maybe it was one hundred? An ideal customer, who yields ten thousand dollars to you, instead of your competitor, may even be worth a three- or four-hundred-dollar bet. And if your odds are one in five or one in three, shoot, maybe it's worth betting a few thousand bucks. Ultimately, whatever number you picked, we have arrived at something important. We have arrived at your marketing Investment per Prospect.

I understand this is far from scientific and that you'll need to run real calculations. The goal here was to just get in the ballpark and for you to see what marketing spend feels right for the ideal customer.

Now that you know the key numbers, the LTV of an ideal prospect, the odds of getting them, and what you are willing to spend, we have the parameters to market differently to get results.

If your Investment per Prospect spend, in this example, was one hundred dollars, I suspect you can instantly see that email marketing or whatever snoozy stuff everyone else is doing in your industry isn't going to cut it. Not by a long shot.

~~~~

While writing this book, I occasionally posed questions to my community about their marketing challenges. This is how I met Linda Weathers. On a Sunday at 3:54 p.m., I posted this:

"I am looking for a story of a business owner who just can't make it happen with marketing and wants to give up. Or has just caved and feels this is the way it needs to be."

Four minutes later, this was her response:

I've spent the last nine months since I started my business trying to figure that out. I gave up and hired someone and nothing happened. I've spent thousands trying to get marketing going. I have worked with dozens of so-called specialists, posting on my own, reading about what to post, so much more. I'm an accountant and tax planner/preparer. It's a business that no one wants to talk about. I save clients up to thirty thousand a year in taxes (my first client, that's exactly what I did for them). I got a website, hired another web designer, and then hired another web designer until I found one who created a website I liked, that covered everything I do properly and professionally. And yet no sales.

I found another "coach" who was teaching people how to do their marketing. I told him I didn't want to learn anymore and spend more money so he agreed to do the marketing for me. He said I have such a great knowledge and that anyone who talked to me would want to hire me. He thought he could get me thirty to fifty contacts to talk to within thirty days. Five months and eight thousand dollars later and I still have nothing. He finally got one person to call me, and it's someone who used to work with me in the past, and I had fired them.

All I do is sit at my computer trying to come up with something to get customers. I am at my computer pretty much from eight a.m. to nine p.m. and sometimes longer. Learning new things that might help me get new

*clients. I really have about eight hours of work a week
with my few clients that I had when it was a part-time
gig. I need to have ten times the clients I have now just
to keep paying the rent. It's very disheartening that
nothing seems to work.*

Linda's response was tough to read. I felt she was taken advantage of by the big, fat marketing lie: when your marketing isn't working, it's because you aren't doing enough of it.

Right away I knew I wanted to help Linda out of this trap, so I asked her to get on a call with me. Five minutes later we met for the first time, on Zoom. She took the call from her bedroom because her sister and her sister's boyfriend had moved into her apartment to help with expenses, so she had little privacy. She also ran her bookkeeping business from that room. And, maybe even tried to sleep in there occasionally, though I suspect it was far from quality sleep.

Over the next hour, Linda explained her situation. She'd been in business for a little over a year and still didn't have a regular client. Not knowing how to find leads, she had invested in three different programs to help her get prospects. Guess how much she spent? How much would *you* have risked on day one? On day sixty? On day two hundred?

Linda spent more than fifty thousand dollars. She had no idea what to expect as far as LTVs go because she had just launched her company, but she was willing to risk her life savings and go into debt to find leads. This is where I get a little heated, because the "marketing experts" who promised her the moon should be ashamed. Bleeding people dry with empty promises is super shitty at best, criminal at worst. It makes me want to toilet paper their house. Right before it rains. You'd help me, right? Yeah, I knew you would.

Linda told me one such expert charged her five thousand a month with the promise of a flood of leads. "I didn't get any leads the first month, so he told me I needed to do more," Linda confessed. "So, I doubled that amount."

A few months and thousands of dollars into this all-too-common horror story, she still didn't have a single lead, and like so many entrepreneurs I work with, she was at the end of her rope. And yet, she still thought maybe she wasn't investing enough. "I am wondering if I just need to stick with it," she said. Yeah, nope.

We are more vulnerable to get-rich-quick bullshit schemes when times are hard, when we are desperate for something, *anything* to work. When we invest in traditional marketing methods such as paid lead gen and paid advertising and get crap results, we often feel as though we have done something wrong. Or that we haven't done enough. Too often we are *made* to feel this way by unscrupulous "experts." It's simply not true.

"Linda, the framework I'm about to teach you will cost you nothing," I told her. "You just have to be willing to do something different."

Grateful and eager, she agreed to follow the Get Different system, with my guidance. Just as I've asked you to do, she first came up with her list of Target One Hundred prospects. Then, we created an out-of-the-box email campaign she could send on her own. Within three weeks, she landed two new clients and one prospect.

Three. Weeks.

Let's compare results. Her traditional lead gen efforts cost her fifty thousand and in nine months landed her zero clients. The Get Different system cost nothing, required fifteen minutes of training, and yielded her two clients and one prospect in just three weeks.

It's important that you understand your Target One Hundred *and* how much you'd invest to land them. Just remember, that number is your max spend. The actual amount can be zero.

Your Turn

If you haven't filled out the first two steps of the Get Different Experiment sheet, do that now. You'll need that information in order to do your first different. Again, you can download it for free at gogetdifferent.com. Or, if you prefer, simply use a piece of scratch paper or keep your experiments in your own journal.

Before you move on to the next chapter, it's important to know which prospects you want to attract, what you want to sell, the intended outcome, and how much you are willing to invest. This clarity will help you target your marketing, thus making it more effective, so please don't skip this step.

Step 1: Objective

Who: Who are you targeting?

What: What are you offering them?

Win: What is the ultimate outcome you intend?

Step 2: Investment

Customer LTV: What is the lifetime value of your customer?

Close Rate Odds: If you put forth your best effort, what are the chances you will land this customer?

Investment per Prospect: Knowing your odds, how much are you willing to invest per marketing attempt to get one of these customers?

	CUSTOMER LTV:_____	NOTES:
STEP 2: INVESTMENT	The typical lifetime value (revenue) of a customer. **CLOSE RATE ODDS:** _____ **OF EVERY** _____ Your expected close rate of engaged prospects e.g. *1 of every 5.* **INVESTMENT PER PROSPECT:**_____ The dollar amount you are willing to risk to land a prospect.	

STEP 2: INVESTMENT—The second stage of a Get Different Experiment, where the customer's lifetime value and associated per-prospect marketing investment are determined.

My Turn

Here's how I filled this section out:

Customer LTV: $28.00

Close Rate Odds: 1:5

Investment per Prospect: $1.00

Notes: The LTV is for one reader only. My royalty (revenue) is $3.50 per book. A lifetime reader will read eight of my books. That is $28. I will create other Get Different marketing plans for engaged readers to deliver other services.

As an author, I sell a physical product—a book. Some formats provide more in royalties and others less, but the average royalty is $3.50 per book.

If I market well to my prospects by being different and attractive, I estimate a one-in-five shot of getting them to buy a book. Remember that the Close Rate Odds are the chances of your prospect getting to your Win. My Win is their buying a book.

I need to break my marketing into a few steps, ensuring a reasonable Direct. So in their first experience with me, I may Direct them to give me their contact information. In a subsequent marketing communication I may ask them to buy the book. Unless it is my mom. Then I just buy the book for her, and tell her it is a gift from my dad.

It's an ego thing.

~~~~~~~~~~~~~~~~~~~~

CHAPTER FOUR

Differentiate for Attention

A week after Jesse Cole proposed to his longtime girl-friend, Emily, they drove to Savannah to watch a minor league baseball game at the city's historic ballpark, Grayson Stadium. At the time, Jesse owned a college-level team, then called the Gastonia Grizzlies. Through loans and investors, he'd scraped together the cash to buy the fledgling team. He looked forward to turning the Grizzlies into a success and starting his new life together with Emily.

"It was a perfect Saturday night. Eighty-two degrees. Clear skies—the perfect day to watch a baseball game," he told me when I talked with him about this book. "And yet, when we walked past the majestic brick columns into the grandstand, we saw maybe two hundred people."

Worse, Jesse explained that the crowd had "dentist energy"—

as though they weren't at a game at all, but waiting to get a root canal.

"I'd never seen a ballpark so empty," Jesse said. "So, after the game, I called up the commissioner of the league and said, 'Hey, if this professional team leaves, we're calling this market right now.' I knew we could transform baseball in Savannah."

Enter providence. Two months later, the New York Mets, which owned the minor league team, demanded a new $38 million stadium from the city, or else they would leave. When the Mets didn't get their stadium, Jesse and Emily got the keys to the old ballpark and a chance to revive another team.

The first few months in Savannah were rough. Despite their business team's best efforts, locals were skeptical. Many people didn't seem to even like baseball. Three months in and just one season ticket had been sold. Jesse and Emily were now broke and had to sell nearly everything they owned—including their bed—to stay afloat.

But they refused to give up. They placed ads in the local newspaper and announced some of the wacky, family-friendly plans they had for the upcoming season: all-inclusive tickets, dancing baseball players, and a breakdancing first base coach. You see, Jesse had a vision. He wanted college-level baseball to be more like the Harlem Globetrotters than the major leagues. He viewed baseball as the act in the center ring of the circus, with near constant entertainment happening all around it. You'd think their plans would receive some attention, but instead, crickets. No one responded. No one responded because *no one noticed.*

"What we needed was attention," Jesse explained. "And to get attention, we needed to do something really different."

Enter providence part deux: they held a contest to name the team. They had a lot of respectable entries from which to choose the name, ideas that *sounded* like Savannah, that sounded like a baseball team *should* sound. The Sailors. The Captains. The Specters. And then, they had one entry that didn't sound like all the rest—the Bananas.

Savannah is not famous for bananas. There's nothing banana-like about Savannah. The name rhymes, and that's about it. But there was one additional thing. One big thing: it was different. Unexpected. So they went with it.

The day Jesse and his team announced the team name, they went from unknown to the talk of the town. Suddenly, the local press wanted to talk to them. Then the national press. They started selling season tickets. Then more season tickets. Before they played a single game, people from all over the world started buying their merchandise.

Opening day of the Savanna Bananas' first season, they were sold out. In fact, they sold out every game of their 2017–2019 seasons.

I've known Jesse for years and shared his million-dollar-debt-to-profitability story in *Profit First* and the major discovery that helped him streamline his business in *Clockwork*. When I was thinking about whom I wanted to talk to about different marketing, he was at the top of my list. Jesse is a *master* of different. His book, *Find Your Yellow Tux*, is a must-read for any business owner who wants to stand out in the crowd. If you read it, you'll immediately understand why he and I are marketing soul mates.

In the summer of 2020, when all of the sports teams had shut down or curtailed activities due to COVID-19, his team was the only one that figured out how to keep ticketholders engaged. In fact, despite the pandemic, the Savannah Bananas still had a profitable year. Compare that to Major League Baseball, which lost $4 billion during the same time period by trying to keep to "business as usual" when people couldn't go to games.[1] Jesse attributes all of his success to having an attention plan, not a marketing plan.

"The reality is, everyone has a marketing plan. But how many people have a plan for how they are going to get attention all the time?" Jesse told me. "You win by being different because it gets attention, always."

Until they do business with you, the only thing people will know of you is your marketing, so market accordingly. A good marketing plan is really an amplification of good marketing. If you haven't proved your plan will get prospects' attention, you'll end up amplifying something that doesn't work. You already know you need to master the milliseconds. First come up with an approach that will pass the blink test and get noticed, and then create a marketing plan to roll it out.

In this chapter, I'll share some strategies I use—and one Jesse uses—to come up with marketing ideas that are different enough to get the attention you need to grow your business. Before we get into that, though, I want you to take "genius idea" off the table. Will you stumble on something that could, one day, be considered a genius idea? Sure. The thing is, you don't need to be brilliant, edgy, or supersmart to find your different. And, you don't have to be like me. I'm an oddball. I think of weird stuff all of the time, and I push past my fears to try my ideas out. You don't have to do that. A simple tweak to what you're already doing for marketing could be all you need. So don't set yourself up for disappointment or frustration with the expectation that you must come up with something revolutionary here. Simple, basic, and easy works, as long as it is different.

Try a Different Medium

One of the easiest ways for you to differentiate your marketing is to deliver it using a different medium—different from what you already use, and different from the established norms in your industry. Who says you *have* to do Facebook ads? Or direct mail? Or video? No one, that's who. Okay, most people in your industry say that. But *no one who gets it* does. What I mean to say is, the marketing "experts," the ad gurus, the people at the chamber of commerce meeting who have "been around the block," they are not the boss of you.

Of course, you'll have to consider if your Target One Hundred will actually *see* your marketing when you change mediums. Not all medium shifts will work. For example, coupons sent in the mail to C-suite executives probably won't get to them, although their assistants may take note. Likely, though, they will be tossed in the garbage before they even reach the assistants' desks.

Take this baby step and ask yourself, "What if I simply changed the *medium* I use to deliver marketing?" Sometimes, that simple shift can make all the difference.

To really jog your noggin, here is a sample list of some marketing mediums:

Videos, signs, brochures, direct mail, influencer marketing, print, packaging, outdoor advertising, indoor advertising, phone, website, pay-per-click, search engine marketing, social media, affiliate, email, television, speaking, referral networking, facilitated word of mouth, trade shows, conferences, access point marketing,* PR, listings, endorsements—the list goes on and on.

Simply try a marketing medium that no one else in your industry typically does. If everyone is sending text emails, send video emails. If they don't do direct mail, you should. If they do, do it in a different way. Different happens when you do the atypical.

One of my favorite direct mail stories comes from Kasey Anton. Now the owner of Spark Business Consulting and a Profit First Certified Master, Kasey once co-owned a swanky restaurant in Boston.

"We were located in an alley in the Back Bay," she told me in an email after I asked her for deets. "You had to be somewhat 'in the know' to dine with us, but even with all that razzmatazz, sexy exclusivity, we couldn't put enough butts in the seats during weekdays."

Kasey came up with an idea—an idea her partners hated. She wanted to send a birthday candle in the mail to previous customers who had filled out a comment card with their name,

---

* There is a seemingly endless source of marketing mediums. I came across the concept of "access point marketing" when I was on a flight. Someone named their Bluetooth and Wi-Fi access point on the phone "The CIA." Cute. Every time I tried to go on Wi-Fi I saw "The CIA," and so did everyone else on that plane. So I changed my phone access point to read, "Buy *Profit First* on Amazon." Whenever I am at a reader event (or on a plane), I activate it. It's password protected, because I simply want them to see it and wonder, "What is *Profit First*?" My hope is they will think, "Let me check it out on Amazon to find out." No one else I know does it, for now. So it's different.

address, and birth date. She planned to include a coupon that read "Dinner on us" and offered them a free entrée of their choice.

"My partners thought it was 'low class,' to be blunt," Kasey explained. "I thought it was simply helping someone celebrate their birthday, which is what I loved about hospitality in the first place—celebrations."

Her partners were all about aesthetics and had no marketing plan—at all. "One partner would go to high-end restaurants and nightclubs 'to be seen' and to oh-so-nonchalantly 'invite' people to come to our restaurant. My other partner, the chef, just stayed in the kitchen, believing, 'if you cook good food, they will come.' I was sick of waiting and the bills needed to get paid. So, I did what I felt I needed to do, which was to invest in my marketing idea and see what I could make happen."

From the comment cards her waitstaff collected, Kasey separated birthdays and anniversaries by month and entered them into a spreadsheet so she could easily print labels. Then, she created the offer in Word. "No fine print, no buy-one-get-one-free, no minimum purchase, because I thought everyone was sick of that crap," she explained. (Yup. We're sick of it, Kasey. Sick of the same old, same old, crap.) "I just wanted to say, 'Hey, it's your birthday, and that's awesome. Let me buy you dinner.' Period. The only caveat was the offer was not available on Friday or Saturday nights, when we were usually quite busy."

Kasey assumed that most people wouldn't dine alone on their birthday, so the restaurant would make a little money off the guests who came with them. And they certainly did. The birthday candles created interest (Differentiate) because it wasn't the typical direct mail campaign, and who doesn't light up (ahem) at the sight of a real birthday candle?

"While my business partners sneered a bit at the campaign, not one customer complained. They *loved* it, and their guests couldn't wait to fill out comment cards to get on our lists."

Kasey tracked the ROI on her candle idea. Other than the cost of the comped entrée, the costs were minimal: around two hundred stamps and two hundred sheets of paper, some printer ink, and a few boxes of birthday candles. So, for under two hundred dollars, they ran a promotion that grossed more than eighteen thousand dollars in new business in one month.

Kasey kept up the promotion until she sold her business in 2008. "To this day," she said, "I believe this is the only thing that kept us afloat for as long as it did."

Do you see the power of changing up the medium? And the power of a simple idea?

Mine for Ideas

If you could be a fly on the wall and listen when people talked about your offer, what would that be worth to you? It's priceless, I tell ya. Group brainstorming is one of the best ways to come up with a ton of different marketing ideas and avoid the inherent bias and knee-jerk judgments we tend to place on our own ideas.

You may have tried an exercise similar to this one, in the past. The Idea Mine is a group brainstorm method I created that is part popcorn, part "Mike," part business mastermind rules. I use this exercise with my team and with my clients.

Here's how it works:

1. Gather a group of at least five people who are willing to participate. Try to find people from different backgrounds, outside of your industry.

2. Assign one person to be the facilitator to keep time and to ensure everyone follows the rules. With your group assembled, give them the following info:

   a) A brief description of your ideal avatar (i.e., your ideal customer)

   b) A brief description of your offer and how it serves your avatar

   c) The problem your offer best solves for your avatar

   d) The typical way your competitors market the same or similar offers to your shared prospects

3. Next, get a notebook and pen to jot down ideas. Then, turn your chair away from the group so you can still hear them but they can't see your face. If you are in a virtual meeting, turn off your camera and your microphone.

4. Set the timer for up to thirty minutes. One at a time, taking turns, each person then shares their new and different ideas about how you could market

your offer. As you hear the ideas, write them down—without comment. You won't have time to judge anyway, because once the group gets going, ideas will fly at you pretty fast.

5. The golden rule of the Idea Mine: no one comments about the ideas. Just move on to the next one, or build on the prior one, but never stop. No quiet time allowed, just ideas. The only bad idea is no idea. It's quantity over quality.

6. If the group gets stuck, the facilitator steps in and tries one of the following techniques:

    a) Roadblock Removal: Get rid of all barriers. Ask the group how they would market if there were no limit on time, money, or other resources.

    b) Roadblock Introduction: Create an unexpected barrier to get the group's brains working in a new way. For example, tell them the ideal avatar is blind, or that they live on an island, or they have a secret superpower.

    c) Inspirational Objects: Select an object from the room and ask participants to come up with marketing ideas that include that object in the approach, or that are related to it.

d) Outrageous Thoughts: Ask the group to suggest marketing approaches that are fun, but risky—the type of ideas that could get you into trouble. Sometimes the best ideas start off crazy!

e) What Would They Do?: Ask the group to consider how a famous person—living or dead—might market your offer. Or what if a child marketed it? Or what about an unaligned profession, like a plumber selling pantyhose? Or a pantyhose mannequin selling plumbing? How would they do it?

The Idea Mine exercise is especially helpful for people who have trouble coming up with unique ideas on their own. You certainly won't use all of them, and you might not use any of them as described, but you will absolutely discover a few gems worth pursuing. At the end of this chapter, I'll share a story about how one of my clients used this exercise to come up with a winning idea that helped her achieve her prospect goal in less than two weeks. It really works!

Identify the Ordinary and the Obscure

A super helpful way to brainstorm different ideas is to observe the ordinary, which sparks the extraordinary. This is key. To see color, you need black and you need white. To hear musical notes, you need silence. To market differently, you must know how people market ordinarily.

Step one is easy: Document your industry's typical marketing method. Describe your offer. What are all of the apparent features and benefits, the same features and benefits your competition brags about? If your competition doesn't sell *exactly* what you offer, they likely do sell something similar, otherwise you wouldn't think about them as competition, right? If it helps, conjure up that image of your nemesis. What aspects of their offer would they highlight in their marketing? For example, do they point out the durability of their product? Or their speedy service? When they do feature comparisons, how do they show that their offer is better than everyone else's?

When listing the benefits of your offer, think experience and outcomes. How does your competition show that the competing product they make is serving the client? The benefit is the "so you can . . ." The feature is the unique function, and the benefit is what you gain from that feature. For example, if the feature is "brighter lighting," the benefit is "so you can see farther."

Now, consider the common use for your offer. How does your target market use your product or service? For example, if you sell reflective tape, is it mostly used for construction sites to mark dangerous areas? Or perhaps runners use it on their shoes and clothes so cars will see them better at night.

With your lists in hand, you've noted how the "gray suits" market. Now let's put on your "red suit" and brainstorm a different approach. Constraints trigger creative thinking. Consider the following:

- What if you had to market your product to a specific person you know? What would get their attention if you were somewhere in a crowd of hundreds?

- What if you had to narrow your marketing to include only one feature and one benefit? How could you amplify it so much that the other things were irrelevant?

- What is atypical about your offer? What does no one else talk about?

- What if you could not use *any* of the standard marketing approaches your industry uses? What might you try?

- What are the reasons people should *not* use your offer? What are the things that *most* people won't like? How can those same things be what a *few* ideal prospects would love?

- What doesn't your product do? What features doesn't it have? How does that make your product or service even better?

Let's delve into that last bullet point. Think about your offer's *absent* features and benefits. The goal for this list is quantity, not quality. Just throw a bunch of spaghetti at the wall, so to speak, and later we'll figure out if any of it sticks.

When I called Jesse to get the lowdown on how, despite the entire world canceling live events, the Savannah Bananas managed to have a profitable year during the 2020 summer of COVID-19, I challenged him to a game of Ordinary and Obscure. Looking around on my desk, I chose the first item I noticed: a simple calculator.

"Let's see if we can market the hell out of this," I said.

As Jesse is my marketing soul mate, I knew he'd be game.

First, we listed all of the features and benefits most companies would mention in marketing the calculator: long battery life, lightweight, accurate, easy-touch buttons, etc. The common use is easy: to calculate stuff. Not that complicated.

With the ordinary lists complete, we focused on the obscure. What were the absent features and benefits of this plain old calculator?

This is a good time to mention that my writing partner, AJ Harper, had joined us on this call. I mention this because AJ hates marketing. I mean, she haaaaaates marketing. Though she may disagree, I think the main driver behind her strong feelings is the fear that she's not any good at it. She also has that ingrained fear of standing out. Earlier on the call, she mentioned a few times how coming up with creative, out-of-the-box ideas came naturally to me and to Jesse. (Marketing soul mates. Have I said that enough times yet? Just want to make sure you've got that.) While that's partly true, what's *more* true is we practice. We build our marketing muscle by working on it. Constantly. The trick is easy, and you can practice all the time, too, including now. Ready?

Look at the first thing you see and come up with different marketing ideas. It could be anything. A Royal typewriter from

1937, a bottle of Caymus cabernet sauvignon, or a Xikezan beard straightener brush. Yes, those are the first three things I saw in my office as I wrote this. I know, it sounds like the beginning of a horror movie. The murder weapon? The beard-hair straightener, of course. The victim? Santa.

My point is you can practice your marketing muscle on *anything*. But it can't be something that you create. We can get really ballsy with other people's stuff yet clam up with our own. So, practice making different marketing ideas for other people's stuff. Got it?

Back to Jesse, AJ, and me.

So here we are, trying to come up with a brilliant new way to market a four-dollar calculator no one *ever* notices, and AJ mostly listens to us riff and occasionally laughs (or rolls her eyes) at our wacky ideas.

Then, suddenly she says, "Well, a calculator doesn't have a GPS. We use the calculators on our phones, but our phones have a GPS." Great point, AJ! There is often just as much power in the features that you *have* as the ones that you *don't*.

We ran with that suggestion and considered the biggest benefits of that "nonfeature." Simple enough: you can add stuff up without being tracked by the gub-or-ment. And when you combine that obscure "nonfeature" with the ordinary feature of a long battery life, well, now you've found a new target customer: survivalists. If you sold calculators, and that avatar was not a good fit for you, then consider how the same "missing" feature would benefit your ideal avatar.

See what brainstorming together can do? Even a person who *hates* marketing and is *really* skeptical about finding a unique way to market something can come up with an idea worth pursuing.

Discover Your "Est"

You already know what happens when you focus on out-bettering your competition—bubkes, that's what happens. Again, because it bears repeating: *Better is not better. Different is better.* Your company likely operates differently from your competitors, better than your competitors, but that distinction alone is not enough to get noticed. First, you need attention. Once you have that, all the reasons you are better than everyone else in your industry have an impact.

The different (there's that word again) thing about the Get Different marketing system is it starts with attention. You'll find amazing books, systems, and strategies—including some I highly, highly recommend, such as *Building a StoryBrand* by Don Miller, *The 1-Page Marketing Plan* by Allan Dib, *Purple Cow* by Seth Godin, and *Duct Tape Marketing* by John Jantsch—and your business will greatly benefit if you use them. This book, though, is different (cha, cha, cha). This book is about mastering the initial milliseconds where either you win the prospects' eyes, or you don't. Without eyeballs on it, an attractive message does nothing.

Now, a little voice in your head may be saying, "Yeah, but, Mikey-Mike, our stuff is better than better. Our stuff actually is the best." Look, I'm not going to dispute the little voice. You may be the best! But being the best is not going to get you the attention you need to generate leads at your command. Being the best supports word of mouth, but marketing differently puts you in charge of lead flow.

In addition to a product or service "best," there's another

"est" that *will* help you get noticed. It is the message or positioning that no one else in the industry can claim. It is the Superlative Marketing Technique.

The hot sauce market is a competitive one to say the least. As I considered some for a dinner we hosted, I found more than one hundred twenty brands, not including their countless flavors. Altogether, one quick search yielded more than five hundred hot sauces. There was Torchbearer, Angry Goat, Bravado, Puckerbutt, Tahiti Joe's, Iguana, Original Juan, Ring of Fire, Ghost Scream, Crazy Jerry's, Bone Suckin' Sauce, Lottie's, Blind Betty's, Ole Smoky, Stubb's, Texas Pete, and Tabasco. Unless you are a true hot sauce connoisseur, you likely recognize few of these brands. Probably Tabasco, the incumbent in the hot sauce market. They are the default when overwhelm presents itself. To beat them you must market differently. All these other brands are different, many are better than Tabasco hot sauce, and a few are categorically great. But none of that matters unless you have an est marketing strategy. And that is exactly what Frank's RedHot did.

Founded in 1918 by Jacob Frank, RedHot made a mild hot sauce. You probably didn't grow up eating it. But you may have heard their genius marketing campaign. It is so successful that as of the writing of this book, Frank's still regularly runs TV and radio spots. The commercial features "Ethel," an elderly "call it as you see it" foodie. When Ethel is asked about Frank's RedHot, she says, "I put that sh*t on everything." Just imagine your lil' ol' grandma saying that.

Grandma talking about hot sauce and saying that she puts that sh*t on everything is different. Kind old voice, talking like a trucker. That is different. That is the crazi*est* thing in the hot sauce space. Frank's RedHot nailed the est, and instead of purchasing the standard Tabasco safe bet, I bought Frank's Red-Hot. It was marketed differently, so I noticed. I bought the est. Honestly, I don't put that sh*t on everything, but knowing Ethel says I can, I buy more.

The est is the superlative of something. Your marketing can be the craziest or weirdest or funniest. Or it can be the sincerest or deepest. It simply needs to be the most in its category. Extremes are noticeable and memorable.

Chances are you can pinpoint the time in your life when you were the coldest. For me it was when I did the fabled Polar Bear Plunge at Coney Island. You can remember the time in your life when you were sickest. You can recall the biggest accomplishment you have had. The greatest vacation you have had. Those are all unique ests. But it is hard to recall the hundreds of times you were "pretty cold" over the last twenty years. Or the countless times you were kinda sick with the sniffles. The est gets noticed. The est gets remembered. The almosts, kindas, and pretty-muches are white noise and forgotten. If you want your prospects to notice and remember you—and for all that is holy, you do—then you can use the est to accomplish just that.

What is your marketing est? It isn't something I can tell you. It surely isn't copying your competition. It is for you and you alone to decide. The nice news is finding it is really simple. Here is how you get started.

A simple web search of "words ending in est" results in thousands of words, which would satisfy even the *persnicketiest* of wordsmiths. Below are some of my faves; I'm giving you one for every letter in the alphabet. But here's the deal: as you go through the list, ask yourself which is an amplification of who you are already, naturally. And if you are in the marketing department, what est most represents an amplification of your company's values? Frank's RedHot is an amplification by being the unapologetic-est. The Savannah Bananas' amplification is by being the funnest baseball team in the world. Your best est is the max of you.

Absurdest

Brawniest

Cheekiest

Deadliest

Edgiest

Filthiest

Gooiest

Hokiest. (I had to do it. Go, Hokies! Non–football fans can use "hottest." UVA fans can choose "haughtiest." Ouch.)

Iciest

Junkiest

Kindest

Leakiest

Mouthiest

Naughtiest

Oddest

Perkiest

Queasiest

Roomiest

Silliest

Tannest

Unluckiest

Vastest

Woodiest

Xeric-iest. (I don't know what it means, either, but my environmentalist son, Tyler, said it while on a hike, so it's gotta be real.)

Yummiest

Zaniest

Which one of these or some other est word could you claim as your unique marketing angle? Without changing a thing in what you do, how can you now describe its merits differently using the est? Create your own est list from the "your different" exercise you did at the end of Chapter 2. Your best ests (say that ten times fast) reside there. Share your list with your team. Which est words describe your company differently? Which est words amplify what your company already is? Once you've figured that out, what medium (e.g., email campaign, mailers, calls, trade shows, tattoos) could showcase that quality? How can you refine your messaging to make sure that your ideal prospects notice your est?

Blend It

For Different Doers you typically want—*hold on!*

Wait a second.

Before I continue, I want you to realize we just had a moment. Me and you. A moment! Do you realize you're officially a Different Doer now? That's a big deal and here's proof: What does DAD stand for? Right! "Differentiate" ("Different" is also acceptable), "Attract," and "Direct." Nailed it. One more test: What question do you ask of every marketing piece forevermore? Righto! "Does DAD approve?" You will never look at marketing the same way again, thanks to your DAD. Ha! Plus, you get all the inside jokes, my newest marketing soul mate. Yeah, we're kinda soul mates now.

Enough bonding, let's get back to work.

As a Different Doer, you typically want to study how the industry is currently marketing so you can avoid the same ignorable noise. With the Blend technique, you want to study people outside your industry to market, at least in part, the way they do. What is already happening for another community has potential to be new and different for yours. So when studying marketing, always—and I mean *A* to the *L* to the *W-A-Y-S*—*always* study how people market outside your market. There is gold in them thar hills. One of the best ways to make sure you don't fall in line with your competition is to fall in line with a completely different industry's marketing. It is the best form of R & D. You know, Rip Off and Duplicate.

I'm old enough to remember when banks started adding a drive-through window. Where do you think they got that idea? From fast-food restaurants. Now, that's a change in the service, but you can apply the same blend technique to actual marketing. For example, McDonald's used toys as a powerful marketing tool. Children begged Mom or Dad to go to McDonald's just for the cheap plastic toys. Vernon Hill, the founder of Commerce Bank, used a similar marketing technique. Noticing how often dogs, not kids, rode shotgun, Hill had his team give out dog treats to customers coming to the drive-through. Now it wasn't the kiddo nagging to go to McDonald's, it was Pavlovian-trained dogs barking and drooling when passing by a Commerce Bank. Hill sold his bank for a transaction valued at $8.5B, as in billion, to TD Bank in 2008.

Let's do some blend marketing for your business and get the next 8.5 Bs in *your* pocket. Let's say you own a vacuum manufacturer. Most marketing for vacuums is on television—the half-hour infomercial in which two actors vacuum up all sorts of weird stuff that probably would never end up on your floor, unless you lived in the back room of an infomercial studio. I mean, who spills dry rice on the ground, pours red wine over it, sprinkles it with dirt, and puts a cherry on top? The ShamWow guy, that's who! By now you've already learned that you are *not* going to try to make a better infomercial that shows how your vacuum can suck up even weirder stuff. Nope. You're going to be different. So, you look to how other companies in different industries market their stuff for inspiration.

Let's take pharmaceuticals. We've all heard the long list of deadly side effects at the end of the commercial, narrated cheerily over an image of a person running through a field of daisies. You know what I am talking about: a young woman spins in a meadow and throws her kid in the air, while the voice-over guy says, "Can cause sudden massive heart attacks. May cause your innards to turn into boiling stew. But hey, you won't have dry eye anymore." Taking a page from their book, you could create a parody of those commercials and come up with hilarious "side effects" of using your vacuum. May cause your mother-in-law to hug you. Might inspire your children to help with chores. Has been known to find the earrings your husband's mistress left behind. See? Funny. Now *that* commercial would get noticed.

Another awesome version of blend technique is called the Profession Pick. It is an extended version of one of the "get unstuck" suggestions from the Idea Mine exercise. Consider how the following types of people might approach marketing your offer:

Your mother, grandmother, or mother-in-law

Religious leaders

Flight attendants

Tarzan (Remember, he knows very few words, but is still very "charismatic" . . . when his shirt is off, or so my wife tells me.)

Mixed martial artists

Lifeguards

Pilots

Bartenders

Farmers

TV hosts

Exotic dancers

Librarians

Clowns

And the ever-so-rare exotic dancer librarian clown

Blend techniques unlock parts of your brain you didn't even know you had. Try it in a group and see what you come up with—but skip the exotic-dancing librarian clown. It's just too weird. And if it is not too weird for you, I think you just found your est. *You* are the weirdest.

Change the Label

If I tell you I'm a lawyer, I can shut my piehole right then and there. You know what a lawyer does. It is a common label and gets its point across fast and efficiently. The problem is the label paints an instant picture in your prospect's mind. A common, standard picture. A lawyer is a lawyer. More common noise, so that just by saying what you do, you instantly put yourself in the zone of a marginalized commodity. Until you change the label, in the prospect's mind you are more of the same—unnoticeable. A truck driver is a truck driver. A landscaper is a landscaper. A personal trainer is a personal trainer. And an accountant is an accountant. Until they are not.

Martin Bissett is the founder of Upward Spiral Partnership, a consulting firm that specializes in helping accounting professionals land more clients. Although he is an accountant himself, he doesn't use that label. Instead, he's a "Knowledge Partner." Now, he's not competing against other accountants, or the ever-popular "trusted advisers" in his industry. He's a one-man show, the only Knowledge Partner (KP, for short) around. A different label is the quickest and freest way to differentiate yourself from the rest of the competition. It doesn't need to be radical or extreme, just vastly different from the majority.

What label could you use that is different from the common labels in your industry? A few words of warning: lofty titles will fail you because they are commonly used. The Queen of Social Media or the Czar of Accounting or the World's Best Hamburger have all been used a billion times. Don't do common. Do new. Get different.

Find Opposites and Loopholes

Opposites and Loopholes is a simple technique that can generate some of the best different marketing ideas. First, make a list of the standard aspects of your offer and your industry. You can pull key points from the Ordinary and Obscure exercise. What is standard about your industry with respect to how you market, deliver your offer, and talk about your business?

Then consider what the rules of your industry are. What does everyone do (or not do), without question? What is *never* allowed? What is expected? What is a given?

Then, look at each standard on your list and think of the opposite of each rule and think of the loophole. Would taking the opposite approach work for your Get Different marketing style? Would rocking the loophole get you noticed?

I used these techniques myself to great effect. I noticed that it was extremely hard to get my books listed next to my contemporaries on Amazon. It was a rare occasion that the Amazon algorithm would display my book as a suggested one when you were looking at, say, *Outliers* by Malcolm Gladwell. But I found a loophole.

Amazon has a section called "Videos for this product" on

the page near the author biography section. Of the millions of eyeballs looking at the book every year, some portion scroll down the page to read more. And by uploading my honest review of Malcolm Gladwell's book, now I'm getting sixty seconds or so of his readers' attention. And wouldn't you know, I am in my office with my books proudly showcased on the shelf. The viewer sees a unique display of my books behind me (Differentiate), while getting the content they seek (Attract), and the trigger to investigate these other books because of curiosity (Direct).

And here's the thing: I just shared one of my Get Different strategies with you and with everyone else who reads this book. The "risk" I run is you and other readers, who also sell stuff on Amazon, replicate the process. This will dilute my videos. But you know what? That is okay. That is the game. All those videos will wipe each other out and become white noise. Until that happens, I will keep doing my Get Different video strategy on Amazon. When it *does* happen, I will be using strategies I have discovered in other Get Different Experiments.

Think Like a Reporter

One of the primary strategies Jesse Cole and his team use to come up with ideas is to think like a reporter. "When we vet ideas, one of the first questions we ask ourselves is, 'Is this newsworthy? Is this a story in itself?' If the answer is yes, we'll try it."

The great example of this is the story that opened this chapter—the naming of the Savannah Bananas. That was just different enough, just controversial enough, to get the attention of main-stream media *and* social media (more on that in Chapter 5). Importantly, it was attractive to the right people. And the directive is built in: get curious, go to the Savannah Bananas website to see what is going on, and tell your friends about this crazy name for a baseball team.

Jesse quickly followed up that strategy with another newsworthy idea: the Bananas announced their team mascot—Split—at a local elementary school. They knew local media would show up for a big pep rally; hundreds of kids going wild for a dude in a banana costume is just good TV. Jesse has a knack for this sort of thing and, over the years, succeeded at getting attention from media all over the world. The Bananas have made the most appearances by a minor league baseball team or all-star baseball team on ESPN—ever. And that kind of attention has generated direct ROI. For example, when President Barack Obama's second term came to a close, the Savannah Bananas publicly offered him an internship. Because that got media attention for the team, they sold more merchandise that day than any other day that month—and it was the off-season.

When you brainstorm your own list of ideas, think like a reporter. What would get the media's attention? A good, unique story. A story with unexpected visuals. A story with unexpected outcomes. Any approach that could get noticed by the media will surely help you get noticed by your ideal prospects, even if the media outlets don't pick it up.

Say, "Yes, and . . ."

Have you ever seen the television show *Whose Line Is It Anyway?* It's a hilarious show in which actors trained in improv take suggestions from the host or the audience and make up scenes—and sometimes songs—on the spot. Improv is a form of unscripted live theater in which most of the show is created spontaneously and collaboratively. One of my favorite bits is when the performers are given an object, like a pitchfork or a beach ball, and have to quickly rotate ideas for what else that item could be. A foam pool toy becomes a phone, a bazooka, a mustache. Simply by asking themselves, "What else could this be?" they come up with different interpretations of an ordinary thing.

This seems like an easy-enough game, but the actors *could* mess it up—if they questioned their own ideas, or another actor's ideas. You see, at the heart of improv is a willingness to take what is handed to you and run with it, to accept it and build on it. It's a rule of improv called "yes, and . . ." It allows for the flow of ideas to continue, and it's the reason why it's so much fun to watch—and do—improv. If instead an actor said, "Yeah, but . . . ," it would interrupt the flow and kill the scene. The moment you question yourself or others, it's over. It's like a kink in the hose that slows your steady flow of water to a disappointing trickle.

My wife, Krista, and I took an improv class at the New Jersey School of Dramatic Arts. After watching her pull off a perfect performance of Dracula reading *Little Miss Muffet* to a group of kindergarteners, our instructor, Bob Sapoff, threw a scenario at me.

"You're an ant taking his dog for a walk in the woods. Go!"

An ant? A freaking ant? I was expecting something at least *close* to human. A zombie, maybe. Or a giant. Not a six-legged insect with a fat ass.

Rather than follow the golden rule of improv, "yes, and . . . ," I did "kinda, but . . ." I didn't want to crawl around on the floor and pretend to be dragged through the forest by a dog, so I made my ant massive. I reset the ant to match what I had already envisioned. I denied the idea. I failed to go with the flow.

As soon as Bob realized my ant would be the size of my aunt (see what I did there?), he said, "Don't do it. Doooon't you do it."

I did it anyway. Even the mighty Sapoff couldn't save me from myself. The bit didn't work. The dog taking a leak on my megaant was the concluding fault. I had created a literal piss ant. Pathetic.

Within seconds, the improv was over and I sat down in my chair in shame because I had ruined the opportunity—and because my wife retains bragging rights for the rest of her Dracula Muffet life.

The "yes, and . . ." rule requires you to build on what you have. It would have been so much better if I went with the ant walking his dog, and maybe gave that ant a Napoleon complex. And maybe imagined his dog was a Great Dane. And then played the scene, clinging to a leash for dear life while shouting commands. Yeah, yeah, yeah. Coulda, shoulda, woulda.

As you brainstorm different marketing ideas, remember to stay open. Don't shut a notion down with your own version of "kinda, but . . ." or "that won't work, 'cause . . ." or "we already tried that." Your very human instinct to try to fit in and conform to what's expected can overtake you, and then before you know it, you'll have modified it into oblivion. Kick around possibilities, without judgment or modification. Make a see-through billboard sign. Use scent marketing to promote your professional services. Have your gas station attendants dress in old-fashioned attire and provide a service commensurate with it. Be the tiny ant being waved around in the wind by the mega-dog and see where it takes you. The views from that vantage point are amazing.

Make Space and Time for Different

In the back room at our offices in Boonton, New Jersey, you'll notice a sign that reads THE MAD LAB. This is ground zero for making different happen in my business. It is the source of inspiration, ideas, and challenging the status quo.

To get in the mood, we placed a mannequin wearing a lab coat, aptly named Abby Normal,* in the corner of the room. Spare lab coats await anyone who enters. We all behave differently when we are in costume, so why not? One wall is covered with dry-erase board material. A massive corkboard hangs on another wall. Yet another is wallpapered with countless random words. Another wall has a shelving system to collect and store ideas from other companies, brands—anybody. A table sits at the center of the room, where we discuss ideas around a lava

---

* Shout-out to Mel Brooks and crew who created one of the funniest movies of all time, *Young Frankenstein.*

lamp. The carpet is a twisting optical illusion, a disco ball hangs from the ceiling, and Mr. and Mrs. Potato Head are randomly moved around the room and placed in compromising positions, like an R-rated Elf on the Shelf.

No matter how much space you have, whether you work at home, in a cubicle, in your car, in a sweet office, or in a giant warehouse, create your own version of the Mad Lab. Make room for creative, out-there ideas to appear out of thin air, to grow, and to thrive. Even a caddy with colorful pens, notepads, and weird fidget toys will remind you to make space and time for different. Consider the caddy as your Get Different Experiment lab kit.

Stay True to Who You Are

I have a goofy sense of humor that not everyone appreciates. I like puns, and bathroom humor, and screwball comedy stuff (#captainobvious). Some of my jokes fall flat (#ouch). Admittedly, some of them just plain ol' suck (#doubleouch). I get it—different jokes for different folks. It's not a big deal if your buddy thinks something is funny and you don't. As an author, though, my unique sense of humor can taint a reader's view of me. Most of my readers love it. Sometimes my humor turns off the "life is too short to laugh" reader, but they soldier through because they need the content to help save or grow their businesses. More times than I can count, I've been called out for not being "serious enough" to write about profitability, systemization, organic growth, and so on. Less often, my style enrages readers. I mean, they *reallllllllly* don't like it. They are outliers, but still; it gets to me.

Like every person on this planet, I struggle with fear of rejection. How much *me* is too much? Almost every business book I've read is deadly serious and quite frankly, despite their insightful content, can be a yawn-fest (to me). My heart screams to make the reading experience fun, but I can become too fraught with fear to go full out, to push on with who I am for the concern of my readers walking away.

This fear of the risk of being "too Mike" came to mind when I attended a party at the home of a very popular author. Although his work is mainstream, his core community is a specific population with specific beliefs. It was a great party, and I was blown away by the author's kindness and hospitality.

A small group of us capped off the night with vintage whiskey and fine cigars. Even our stogie bud Gabe Piña would have been impressed. Then, when we were about to take a departing group picture, the author said, "Hold on. I need to hide the whiskey. My community won't like it."

"Wow," I thought. "This guy sells a huge amount of books. Maybe I need to rethink how I market myself. Maybe putting up a facade persona actually helps. Maybe different means being different from who you really are."

Yeah, that thought lasted about two seconds, and then I shook my head. I was pissed—

Pissed at myself for even giving it a moment's thought. This author, who had sold and continues to sell an ass-ton of books, marketed in a way that was not true to who he really was. If being in the big leagues requires me to be a big fake, small fake, or kind of in-between fake, well that's just not gonna work for me. Look, I'm not trying to be all judgy-judge about this author. But I *will* judge myself for pretending to be someone I am not. I am who I am. Your opportunity to market differently is to simply be more you, authentically.

Apparently, you can fake it and still make it. But then you will have to live a double life, hiding aspects of yourself from the people you serve. That disconnect will always be there.

I shared the whiskey anecdote with you because I want you to see that, sometimes, I'm afraid to be different, too. Of course I want the world to see me favorably. None of us want to face criticism for doing something people don't approve of. But I can't live with my own criticism of myself for behaving like someone I am not. The risk of authenticity is worth it. More than that, it is necessary. Being disingenuous with your community is a much higher risk. It's the risk of their finding out, and you have to go on TV and do that big televangelist crying apology thing, sobbing through your words: "I'm a sinner. I'm a sinner." Or even worse, it's the risk of getting away with it as you slowly lose your soul.

While writing this book, I received an email from Skylar Bennett, the owner of Tough Apparel, who had read one of my books. The second line of his email read, "I'm not sure I've ever laughed and cried simultaneously so much during the first thirty pages of any book, ever before in my life." Yeah, okay. Message received. Goofball Mich-alo-shits for-ev-ah!

Do different. Be consistently, unapologetically you. The people who need you will be eternally thankful for it. And the people who don't need you? They'll be grateful they didn't buy into a fake.

~~~~

Ernestina Perez needed fifteen new clients to hit her revenue goal, and she had no idea how to get them. Better said, she had no *new* idea how to get them.

A therapist in Chicago, she had started her own practice in May of 2019, Artfulness Counselling. At the time, she worked full-time at a different practice and with her private clients on weekends.

In July, she brought on her first employee, another therapist. To keep a steady flow of clients, she relied on Zocdoc, a lead gen service that charged three thousand dollars per year, per therapist.

"We found that most clients sought us out because we were Latina," Ernestina told me in an interview for this book. "We spoke Spanish and we understood Latinx culture. They could identify with us."

In the spring of 2020, Ernestina changed the name of her practice to Latinx Talk Therapy. She wanted to have a greater impact on her community, which meant she wanted to expand. Adding fifteen new clients would give both her and her employee a full case load and enough cash flow to make her next hire.

Her ideal clients are Latinx people who were born in the US or who immigrated when they were very young, so they had adopted American culture. For most, their family speaks Spanish at home, and it's the first time anyone in their family has gone to therapy.

"I didn't know how to get Latinx clients. I was just lucky that they occasionally found me," she explained. "We wouldn't get them through our paid listing in *Psychology Today* or Zocdoc. I wondered, 'Where am I going to get all of these referrals?' I hadn't seen another private practice that was niched for a specific group of people. I couldn't follow a system that worked for another niched practice. How would I grow without knowing how to do it?"

That spring, Ernestina joined a group of entrepreneurs at one of my Get Different sessions. She volunteered to be a guinea pig for the Idea Mine exercise. After she stated her target client goal to the group, she turned off her Zoom video, muted her microphone, and furiously took notes as other entrepreneurs in the group shared ideas on how to market her business differently, which triggered her own ideas. By the end of twenty minutes she had forty new strategies to market her practice immediately.

When she shared her list with me, I challenged her to try a Get Different Experiment to test one of the strategies. I encouraged her to start with video, because (1) it was uncommon for therapists to do it, (2) it took very little (as in no) money to create, and (3) it required very little time. The key for Ernestina, and for you, is to start and build the different marketing muscle immediately. Do different marketing, in small, low-cost, low-effort ways to get started. The biggest hurdle you will face is the "courage" to do different. And the goal is to test at a low cost and with low effort, to prove it works (or doesn't).

"I was talking with my sister about making videos that would be different," Ernestina told me. "She watches a cable show called *90 Day Fiancé*, and she said, 'Why don't you give advice for the couples on the show?'"

Ernestina had never seen the program, and when she watched it, she understood the potential. In one particular episode, an American man and a Colombian woman were in conflict due to cultural differences. A minute in, the scene erupted into an argument, and the woman threw a glass of water in the man's face.

"When I watched, I understood where the Colombian girl was coming from. Her fiancé was a machista," Ernestina said. "My sister asked me how they could go from having issues to a healthy relationship, and I said, 'Oh, *that* I can do!'"

She recorded a video of herself watching the couple argue and shared insights about how to better handle those issues: "Therapist Reacts — *90 Day Fiancé* Jennifer and Tim." Let me tell you, that video is hilarious. Watching Ernestina try to maintain professional decorum when a woman throws water in her boyfriend's face—riveting. She posted the video on Instagram.

"I didn't know how the video would convert to therapy. Therapists are supposed to be professional, subdued listeners. This required me to be me. And I was afraid that someone watching the video would be disappointed that I am reviewing a reality TV show," she explained. "But sure enough! People saw me, realized they needed help with moments when their emotions get the best of them, and called for appointments."

Her *90 Day Fiancé* review got almost twenty-five hundred views in one week. Her standard commercial video explaining her services got less than six hundred views since it was posted over a year ago. She planned to create more "Therapist Reacts" videos but stopped because she had exceeded her goal, with one video. A test video, no less. Her practice had received thirty-one inquiries from people who watched the video and she booked twenty-three new clients—eight more than she needed.

According to the United States Department of Labor's Bureau of Labor Statistics, more than 552,000 mental health professionals practice in the US today. Ernestina is one in half a million. Traditional math suggests that the odds of success are against her. Those who pick four random-number lotteries have better odds of winning.

Yet, within one week of doing a Get Different Experiment, Ernestina achieved a growth goal she struggled with since the start of her business. She has expanded her team, her client roster, and her brand recognition, and has plans to grow a group practice to fulfill her mission. She serves a community that needs her, because they see her now. She has taken on the responsibility of marketing differently so that she can serve exceptionally. And she didn't have to radically change her business or spend a fortune on marketing help. She pulled it off by trying one different approach.

You, too, must take complete control of your own lead generation. As you've already learned, word of mouth is great, but you can't control it; you are dependent on your customers, waiting for them to talk you up. It is not throttleable, it's haphazard. Paying for leads, as Ernestina did, gets you in front of a small group of people who are solicited by a large group of competitors; it can work, but it can get really saturated, and really, really expensive. And, with paid listings you are at the mercy of that site's algorithm, templates, and rules.

Paid advertising is the fine for not being different, and a lack of consistent prospects is your prison sentence.

Why did Ernestina's free approach work over the tried-and-true, expensive lead gen service she utilized? It worked because it was different for that market. Different enough to get the immediate attention of her desired demographic, relatable enough to keep them engaged, *and* compelling enough to make them reach out to her. That's the power of different; it simply needs to be different in the context of people seeing it. Yeah there are millions of videos out there, with all sorts of things. But for the Latinx community in search of a therapist, watching a video like Ernestina's was different. Therefore it wins.

Why did Reddit's marketing campaign work, even though it only cost five hundred dollars—for stickers? People stuck the company's smiling alien logo on laptops, and posted pics on social media. At the time, stickering was radically different *in the way* their intended community loved. Now laptops are covered with stickers, making them unnoticeable. Reddit was among the first to have customers "deface" their laptops with stickers. That was different. That won.

Why did Beyoncé's self-titled 2013 album earn her a *Guinness World Record* for the fastest-selling album on iTunes? Because she dropped it *without any advance promotion*. She delivered it in a different way, and that approach was so out of the norm, it *became* her promotion.

You don't have to be Reddit or Beyoncé to do different. You can become the next Reddit or Beyoncé by doing different. You don't have to be super special, extremely creative, or exceedingly smart. You don't have to be naturally good at brainstorming ideas. You don't even have to be experienced in business. In fact, if you think you're clueless about marketing, you already have a major head start over those who *do* think their marketing is one of their strengths. Remember that sea of gray suits, everyone looking for a soul mate? They all think they know something special about marketing, when all they really know is how to market like everyone else.

Doing different is not for the chosen few creatives who are blessed with a bottomless bowl of brilliant ideas. You can learn how to do this. It is a simple process. That awesome thing you worked so hard to build, to create, to launch—you *can* get prospects to notice. While it may feel risky to do Get Different Experiments, the only real risk is in not doing them.

When Ernestina made her video, she was really nervous. "At the time, I was still getting used to public speaking," she told me. "I had to challenge myself, though, because my community needs me. I had to step up."

When she recorded the video, she felt as though she might throw up. "I thought, 'What if I make this video and people don't take my company seriously?' I was getting in my head." The greatest risk, she realized, was not being seen as a joke. The greatest risk was not being seen.

Because she stepped up, because she "took a chance" and came up with her own "spin," Ernestina's confidence level for "getting different" has increased—and so have her opportunities. Since she posted the video (I remind you, one video—one stinkin' video), she has been contacted by several organizations who want her to speak, including HispanicPro, a networking group for professionals in the Chicago area. And, this won't be a shocker, she made more videos.

"Now I have the skills to come up with ideas," she said. "I know the strategies. I know that when I did do something different, the community that I serve really liked it. I just have to keep reminding myself that getting noticed works and to do it again."

You feel like a novice? You think marketing is not your thing, or that you really suck at it? Perfect. You are ready to break "the rules." Let's get to work.

Your Turn

This is the brainstorm phase, and it's crucial that you stay open to possibilities at this stage. As you work through this book, remember you don't have to come up with a "major" or "big" idea. Ask yourself what you can do that is a simple change, yet different enough to get noticed, to get people saying in their minds, "I haven't seen that before." Start there—with small, easy differents.

Step 1: Identify three mediums to deliver your marketing that are the most compelling. Here's a partial list from which to draw your answers:

Print

Direct mail

Packaging

Outdoor

Broadcast

Phone

Website

Pay-per-click

Search engine marketing

Email

Social media

Affiliate

Speaking

Referral network

Word of mouth

Trade show

JV promotion

Pro tip: Don't select your medium based on "best practices" in your industry or because "everyone else does it." Consider where you see an opportunity to be different.

Step 2: Start generating different marketing ideas for the medium you chose. Use the techniques you discovered in this chapter to help you get started. Consider a different medium to deliver your marketing. Mine for ideas using the group brainstorm method. Identify the ordinary and the obscure aspects of your offer. Discover your est. Blend your marketing idea with one used by another industry. Change the label. Find Opposites and Loopholes. Think like a reporter and come up with marketing ideas that are newsworthy.

Step 3: Review the ideas you have created and pick your best option. Which one do you feel has the most potential, even if it makes you a little nervous? Give detail to this idea on how it will be different. How will prospects notice your different marketing? How will the medium be used? Push yourself outside of your comfort zone, but stay within the real-you zone.

Step 4: Lastly, ask yourself, "Does DAD approve" your idea? You will only know for sure through experimentation, but refine your idea as much as you can to ensure it is an unignorable, safe opportunity with a specific and reasonable directive. Check off each DAD element when you are confident your idea achieves it.

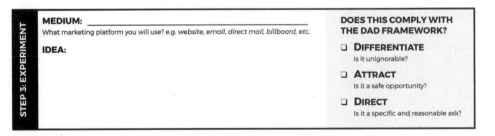

STEP 3: EXPERIMENT—The third stage of a Get Different Experiment, when the different marketing concept is proposed and evaluated for compliance with the DAD Marketing Framework.

My Turn

As I continue to work on my own newest Get Different Experiment, I have already determined the Who (reader), What (*Get Different* book) and Win (buy a copy). I have also determined that the twenty-eight-dollar LTV of a customer easily justifies, in my mind, a one-dollar Investment per Prospect. Now I need to Get Different this opportunity.

First, I work through my idea. A direct mail campaign would get noticed, but it will be difficult to keep my investment under one dollar per prospect. Video is cheap and easy. But it is a common medium for most authors in my genre. I noticed that almost all authors have a standard bookshelf behind them. What if I did a radically different bookshelf, something no one else has, and featured my books on it?

Once I have my idea, I add it to my Get Different Experiment sheet:

> <u>Medium:</u> All videos prerecorded and live broadcast.

> <u>My idea:</u> An unexpected bookshelf.

> <u>Differentiate:</u> At this stage of building an experiment, I focus on Differentiate and make a best guess at Attract and Direct. It does

Differentiate, so that is checked off. The key is that "everyone" has a traditional bookshelf display. That is the one thing I must avoid. A search for "unique bookshelves" yields amazing designs. One that looks like the United States, another that is big letters saying READ (a built-in Direct!), another that is a sideways piano. These are all Different and I think can all work.

A different bookshelf feels right. Now it must be consistent with my brand and keep people engaged in the Attract phase.*

---

* Reminder: I have made a video detailing my bookshelf Get Different Experiment. You can get free access to this and other free resources by visiting gogetdifferent.com.

~~~~~~~~~~~~~~~~~~

CHAPTER FIVE

Attract for Engagement

W e got our asses kicked by some geeks with taped-up glasses.

I started my first company, Olmec Systems, in 1996. At age twenty-three, I left my job as a "computer guy" to open my own business—as a "computer guy." I started with a nothing budget, much like one of our competitors: Geek Squad. Their founder, Robert Stephens, had launched his company two years before mine with just two hundred dollars. (Respect, man. That's my kind of startup.)

In an effort to look professional, I showed up to service appointments wearing a suit. It was always the same ill-fitting number with oversize shoulder pads. I couldn't afford two suits, let alone something stylish (with bigger shoulder pads). But I thought I looked the part. Picture a lanky guy in a big baggy scarecrow suit. 'Twas me. Sometimes, I wore my tan polo with the company logo on it. I was proud of that logo, because I'd paid one thousand dollars for it. Yup, you read that right. One thousand 1996 dollars, which I think is about seven billion in today's dollars. At least that's what it felt like at the time. A thousand bucks was half of my startup capital. I thought that logo would legitimize the company and attract prospects. Mistake number one. Mistake number two was looking like every other lanky computer technician on the planet.

The Geek Squad? They showed up to appointments with dark-rimmed glasses taped in the middle, the most famous "logo" of nerds worldwide. But the uniform didn't stop there. They looked like geeky FBI agents: white, short-sleeved, pocketless dress shirts; black pants (flood pants, high enough to show off their glistening white socks); black lace-up shoes; and a black tie with the company logo pin. They even put that logo on the soles of their shoes so that when they walked on the sidewalks in those hardcore Minnesota winters, they left "Geek Squad" footprints in the snow. Genius! Pure. Different. Genius.

What's more, they didn't call themselves computer techs, or computer guys or gals or whatever. They were double agents, special agents, and deputies of counterintelligence. Geek Squad's founder, Robert Stephens, called himself the Chief Inspector. Me, I called myself the CEO and chief bottle washer. Only later did I realize this is the exact same self-deprecating joke that every other business owner used. Geek Squad had that whole different label thing down pat, while I tried to fit in. That was mistake number three.

To me, their branding looked like a gimmick. I thought they

were a joke, and I wasn't alone. All the competitors in our space laughed at Geek Squad. Were they thinking it was Halloween dress-up time every single day? I mean, come on.

Then, they destroyed us.

Actually, they slaughtered us. Maybe it was *Halloween* (the movie) after all, and they were Michael in the pasty white mask, hacking away at us.

Geek Squad dominated the attention game right from the get-go. They were no more capable than we were and no more masterful at service. If anything, we had a better quality of service. They beat us, and hundreds of other computer companies, by marketing differently. Geek Squad graduated from riding bikes to clients (true story) to actual cars, Volkswagen Beetles painted black and white with the logo on the door. And these different cars ensured they remained the talk of the town. Their uniform became so iconic, in 2000 the Minnesota Historical Society added it to their permanent collection. You won't find any of my scarecrow suits or coffee-stained polos hanging in some museum in New Jersey. Pretty sure you can't even find them at Goodwill.

They key to Geek Squad's marketing game wasn't just that people noticed them. Their marketing drew the attention of the right customers and turned that initial awareness into enduring attraction. Sustained attraction comes from seeing a benefit and feeling appropriate safety in the pursuit of it. At the end of the day, a prospect will be attracted to your marketing as long as they feel they have more to gain than to lose by continuing to consume your message. Geek Squad's whole *Dragnet/Men in Black* vibe instilled confidence in people, because it reminded them of the *actual* FBI. People gave them the benefit of their trust immediately because of the uniforms, and curiosity kept them engaged.

While we, their competitors, laughed at their silliness, customers flocked to Geek Squad. Their getup was fun, made being a geek cool, and made their customers feel safe. Although Stephens developed a system for delivering consistently good computer service—the benefit—they didn't even have to claim they were better than the average Joe (or Mike) at computer repair. They went with different, and better didn't matter.

In 2002, just eight years after he founded the company, Robert Stephens sold Geek Squad to another Minnesota-based company, Best Buy, for $3 million plus a fat share of the future profits. He stayed on with the company and helped it grow to more than a billion dollars in annual revenue. In the end, I sold my first computer company for a few hundred thousand dollars in a private equity deal. Sure, I got a nice cherry on top, but Stephens got the whole damn sundae. I can't say it enough: different wins.

By now, I hope you have a list of different marketing ideas you could try. But remember, it's easy to get excited about a new marketing approach that is sure to get you noticed and then overlook the next step in the DAD Marketing Framework: Attract.

We need to make sure your Get Different marketing will attract your ideal avatar, those prospects you most want to work with and who want the service or product you most want to sell. As you read this chapter, have your list of Differentiate ideas handy and ask yourself, "Will my Get Different marketing make my ideal avatar feel safe?" and "Does my different approach clearly show an opportunity for them?"

What Attraction Influencers Will You Use?

The Attract stage of the DAD Marketing Framework is designed to hold your prospect's attention. You've got to keep winning them over, again and again. The second they deem you uninteresting, you are done. So, to keep them engaged and build enough comfort for them to take the next action, you'll need to consider which Attraction Influencers will do the job.

Among the dozens of books on the concept of prospect attraction there are even more techniques. *How to Win Friends & Influence People* by Dale Carnegie was my first read on the subject, and since then I've discovered and read at least fifty more on the topic. I've distilled the most important and effective of these Attraction Influencers to help you think through your own approach.

- Authority[1]—This is when we have heightened trust for an individual or brand because we see them as a leader in their category. Our default belief is that they have knowledge, expertise, capabilities, or influence greater than ours, and we trust that their opinion relative to their respective space is superior to our own. People who value this are attracted to "rub elbows" with the authority to learn from them and to increase their own social significance. For example, a doctor in an ad for a new drug will likely sell more of that medication than a race car driver would. Authority with perceived applicable expertise is more influential. The race car driver can sell more tires than a doctor.

- Trusted source[2]—This is a person or brand that we already have confidence in and will follow. They are not necessarily in an authority position, but we have had past experiences with them. We have familiarity with a trusted source and can predict how our experience with them will pan out. For example, if your mom has cared for you and she tells you to have chicken soup for your cold, you are more likely to have it than if I told you to have chicken soup for your cold, unless you already have experience with me helping you with your health. Further, if she made that soup for you before, and you loved it, you will likely choose her recipe over one from someone else.

- Repetition[3]—The more we hear a recurring message, the more it attracts. If we repeat the message in our minds, we start to feel as though we came up with it. When we notice the same thought that we had articulated by someone else, or repeated in marketing, we are drawn to it. How many times have you heard the phrase "Better late than never"? Probably a lot—so much that you trust it and it feels true. Is it really better to be late than to never show up? Maybe sometimes, but not *most* times. Is it better to be late to a meeting than never show up? Sure. But it's much better to be punctual. Phrases and "facts" that we repeat often (or hear often) become more trusted purely because they are repeated often enough, even though they aren't always—or ever—true.

- Social significance[4]—We seek to be important and relevant to our community. When something elevates our standing in any capacity—makes us stronger, healthier, cooler, funnier, better—we are attracted to it. If social significance is important to you, a hair product that promises to make you "the envy of your friends" and car ads that assure you that "people will know you're a success even before you open the car door" will appeal to you.

- Alignment[5]—We are attracted to what we already know and feel. Alignment validates us, as we are. An extension of this is purpose/righteousness, which speaks to our purpose and belief system. This plays into confirmation bias—our tendency to favor things we already believe and discredit or ignore things we don't. So, if you have an offer for pre-packaged nutritious meals and you want to attract people who are already invested in their health and wellness, a marketing approach centered around "you are what you eat" aligns with their identity and beliefs. If someone believes that all calories are the same, they will ignore or discredit your marketing.

- Safety[6]—We seek safety and protection from physical harm or discomfort, from financial struggle, and from rejection from our community and our ideology. We are attracted to messaging that makes us feel safe in any of these areas. For example, booking a flight on an airplane that assures you its "hospital-grade air filtration system kills 99.9 percent of bacteria and viruses" makes us feel safer anytime we're packed in like sardines.

- Comfort[7]—A variant of Safety, in which we have an aversion to loss and are attracted to maintaining what we have. We are attracted to things that will assure we can sustain and expand elements of our life and work that we already enjoy. We've all seen marketing that highlights the fact that we "can do it from the comfort of our own home." That one is pretty transparent, right? Marketing that mentions *avoiding or preventing* discomfort also attracts. The roofing material that is impervious to rain and won't let any water into your house protects you from discomfort.

- Expansion[8]—We like to expand the things we already like, own, and believe. People who value their nice car will be attracted to a nicer car; people who value their privacy will be attracted to gaining even more privacy, and so on. When you think about

expansion, think upgrades, such as upgrading ac-
commodations or travel arrangements. Think more,
such as bonuses and extras.

- Belonging[9]—We value being part of a community,
  being loved by our community, and contributing to
  our community. Messages that help us feel a sense
  of belonging are attractive to us. Lady Gaga's community of "Little Monsters" is an excellent example
  of that. By giving her fans the name, she gives them
  a new community and inspires new fans to join.

- Health[10]—We are attracted to things that deliver
  health to us—unless we're talking about gluten-free
  muffins. Or a three-hour spin class. This can be
  physical health, sexual health, mental health, and
  more. If something improves our longevity, strength,
  endurance, and overall well-being, we are attracted
  to it. You hear messages related to health all day
  long: You will be more physically attractive by using
  this piece of equipment. You will be able to be a sexual powerhouse with this blue pill. You will think
  clearer by taking our meditation course.

- Relief[11]—Things that offer us permanent or tempo-
  rary relief from physical or emotional pain are compelling. Humans are wired to gain pleasure and avoid
  pain, and if both are happening at the same time, the

avoidance of pain is usually the winner. Consider that it could also be relief from something simple, such as sitting in traffic too long.

- Beauty[12]—Though no single definition exists, we are, nonetheless, attracted to that which we find pleasing to the senses. When you know how your prospects define beauty, you can amplify it by sharing something that could be viewed as *more* beautiful. This tattoo will show your heritage—for people who see that as beautiful, that is compelling. The color of this top will emphasize your eyes, may be beauty.

- Esteem[13]—We are attracted to things and messages that make us feel valued and recognized. We strive to be recognized for being important and relevant. Esteem is similar to belonging, but with an emphasis on specific importance. So, for example, a prestigious award or accolade, or a special distinction.

Considering what you know about your ideal customer—their values, preferences, and habits—which Attraction Influencers do you think would speak most clearly to them?

Does Your Marketing Match Your Offer?

Outrageous marketing does get noticed, but if it's incongruent with the desired engagement, that outrageousness becomes an oddity and something to be avoided. I witnessed a great example of this while driving to lunch with my good friend Paul Scheiter. As we passed by a nondescript strip mall outside St. Louis, Missouri, we stopped at a red light—next to the Statue of Liberty.

On the corner, a bedraggled guy with bags under his eyes, an epic sneer, and three-day stubble stood wearing the cheapest Statue of Liberty costume you can imagine: green toga, foam crown, and all. He had the look of someone nearing the end of a weeklong bender. To cap it off, a half-burnt cigarette drooped from the corner of his chapped lips; the smoke curled up and twisted around his foam headpiece. He shuffled ten feet up the sidewalk, faced—scratch that, sneered at—a different set of cars for a few seconds, and then shuffled back. In his weathered hands he held a sign that read LIBERTY TAX. FREE TAX CONSULT TODAY.

Although I couldn't help but stare at this train wreck, I did everything I could to avoid eye contact. When the traffic light turned green, we couldn't get out of there fast enough. In my last glance at him, he was putting out his cigarette on the back of the sign. My God!

A beleaguered guy in a Statue of Liberty costume who looks like he would murder the next person he meets definitely passes the Differentiate test. Except he fails the Attract test. A (likely) strung-out (potential) criminal does not instill confidence in tax services. And even if he was just a down-on-his-luck guy trying to make a buck, his appearance was *incongruent with the offer.* Tax consults? With this guy? Or with the person who hired him? I question the professionalism of anyone who thought it was a good idea to put a twenty-dollar costume on the dude and send him out in public. And I'm sure I wasn't the only person driving by that day who felt that way.

Sometimes, an idea that works in one context can turn people off under different circumstances. Remember Kasey Anton's birthday candle story? She kept her restaurant afloat by mailing birthday candles to customers during their birthday month with an offer for a free entrée. It worked like a charm—except in the summer months.

"As it turns out, candles don't travel so well in envelopes when it's hot," Kasey explained in her email to me. "As a matter of fact, by the time they reach their intended destination, they look more like that guy's face that melts off in *Raiders of the Lost Ark*. Not really the look I was going for."

Kasey exchanged the candles for confetti, which didn't work very well, either. Most people don't like to have to clean up confetti from the cracks in their floor. So, she saved the different idea that worked for cooler months and tried another different idea during summer: a handful of colorful deflated balloons.

Sometimes your offer makes sense to your ideal prospect, but puts everyone else off. In the last chapter, I shared the naming story for the Savannah Bananas. That was the first turning point for that business, because it got them the attention they needed to generate interest. The thing is, the name received sharp criticism from the city's sports media, from local baseball fans, and from other team owners. They felt that Jesse and Emily Cole and their team did not take baseball seriously.

Guess what? They didn't. They took *family entertainment* seriously.

When they first landed in Grayson Stadium, Jesse made dozens of calls each day and received the same response nearly every time. "I wanted to introduce myself to the community and get them excited about the next season and all we had planned," he told me. "But when I mentioned baseball, most of them said, 'I don't really like baseball.' They thought it was too long, or too boring, or too long and too boring."

The previous team couldn't fill the seats. Hell, they couldn't even fill a couple of *rows* of seats. Jesse knew that he had to market to families looking for a fun activity, not to baseball fans. So, when they announced that the team name would be the Savannah Bananas—not the Scepters, or the Sailors, or any other "respectable" baseball team name—the criticism from hardcore baseball fans and industry people didn't faze them.

Jesse and his team knew the name would appeal to the exact people they wanted to draw to their games—families looking for a fun activity. People who wanted to be entertained. The kind of people who would want to see the first baseball pep band and a senior citizen dance troupe. So what if they repelled the serious folks? They attracted thousands to fill those stands because their marketing aligned with their offer. I mean, if you buy a ticket to see the Savannah Bananas, you expect to have some wacky fun. And that's what you'll get—with a side order of baseball.

A quick PS for this story—now those hard-core baseball lovers come to the games, too, and they love it. They have discovered that baseball can be even more than baseball. Different done right will attract the right customers. And the right customers can attract *all* the customers.

Consider your Target One Hundred prospect list. What type of Attraction Influencer would appeal to them? For example, Geek Squad attracted customers using both safety and curiosity. Though they failed at it, the Liberty Tax store may have been trying to attract customers by offering a sense of financial comfort. Then, review your list of ideas. Which of them would repel or fall flat for your ideal prospect, and which would attract them?

Is Your Target Customer Tired of It?

The first time I attempted to market Olmec Systems, I sent out a direct mail campaign. I wanted to "elevate" my marketing approach above door-to-door selling, which I sucked at. No really, I did door-to-door. I gave up after half a day. Now, remember, at this point, I'm still trying to do the things that every company does—which is how I ended up with a one-thousand-dollar logo that made zero impact. With no results from the logo (shocker, I know), I made the classic mistake of copying the marketing "best practices" of my competitors. Which, in this case, was to buy a list. Two thousand names at fifty cents a pop came out to—yup, I did it again—*one thousand dollars*. Between that charge, paper and envelopes, and postage, I ended up spending three thousand bucks.

As it turned out, I also sucked at direct mail campaigns. The list company that assured me all of the addresses were current totally lied, because of the two thousand mailers, around a quarter of them were returned. For the remaining fifteen hundred mailers, I got only one response. And it was not pleasant.

The mailer started off with "Dear ____," with the appropriate first name in the blank field. The one that came back was addressed to "Dear Tyrone . . ." I know this because he mailed it back to me, with his name circled in red marker. He added a note that read "Do I know you, asshole?" Apparently, he did, because he knew my nickname.

My target market was business owners, and I had failed to attract them right out of the gate. First, I used a tired marketing technique that landed my expensive mailer in the trash with a lot of other expensive mailers. What's more, by addressing them informally, with their first names instead of Mr. or Ms., I ended up pissing them off. Well, at least, Tyrone was pissed. If you're reading this now, T-man, I'm truly sorry. I can't remember your last name, but you deserved the respect of me using it. Love, Asshole.

My first marketing attempt was a bust because I failed at the first two components of the DAD Marketing Framework, but I think the informal address was the real turnoff. The experience made me fear direct mail campaigns so much that I didn't try them again for another five years. For the record, I use them now for bulk book sales, and it works like a charm because (a) hardly anyone uses them to market books, so they are different, (b) they are designed to attract a very specific readership, and (c) they have a direct call to action. Ask yourself, is your marketing approach tired, or inspired?

Does Your Idea Speak to Your Prospect's Identity?

Can you name the two most powerful words in the English language? In fact, these two words are the most influential in any language. They will get your interest every time. If they were headlined in today's newspaper, I guarantee that you would read the article. If you and I were locked in a conversation, and you overheard even just one of these words, you might continue to look at me, but now you would be listening to what you overheard. Just one of these words pulls you in like a magnet every time. And together they are irresistible. Can you identify them, even one?

You may guess "thanks" or "sale" or "free" or "sex." It is none of those. I mean, well, I guess "free sex" maybe. But no, not even that. The most attractive words, in any language, are a person's own first and last name.

One of the surest ways to get people to notice you and attract them to your offer is by using their name. We always pay attention to our own name. Always. You'll see the use of people's names in all sorts of ways. On nameplates in restaurant booths. During shout-outs on public radio pledge drives. On conference room doors. And man, oh man, if I could have figured out how to get your name on the cover of this book and in these pages, I would have done it. Imagine me saying, "You will always pay attention to _____ _____." (If you want to play along, you can write in your first and last name in those blank spaces.) It looks good, right? I mean, it's your name after all!

People are also attracted to their own image. Podzemka, a club in Moscow, used this to their advantage. Their ideal prospects are Gen Z, a demographic for whom marketing and advertising often falls on deaf ears. So Podzemka came up with the idea to use its target customers' own images to attract them. On its website, a page was added where club-goers could upload photos of themselves and add cool templates and slogans. In this way, the club's prospects were creating ads *for* the club. Gen Z loves to create memes and share pics with each other, so those self-made ads spread on social media like wildfire. After implementing this strategy, Podzemka had a 50 percent increase in traffic to its website.

Beyond a prospect's name and photo, there are other aspects of their identity to consider. We are attracted to images and messages that *affirm* our identity. Take the "Don't Mess with Texas" slogan. I'll bet you didn't know that came from an anti-littering campaign. Unless you're from Texas, in which case, pardon me. I'm sure you *did* know, because you're a Texan and all.

In 1985, the Texas Department of Transportation asked GSD&M, an advertising agency based in Austin, to come up with a slogan to help deal with the state's massive littering problem. They wanted something geared toward men, who littered more often than women, and people who believed that being Texan allowed them to do whatever they wanted with their litter. The firm came up with the phrase "Don't Mess with Texas" in part because they didn't want to use the word "litter." The word "mess" was reminiscent of moms telling their kids to clean up their "messy" rooms.

The campaign ran statewide on road signs, on television and radio ads, and in print ads. Between 1987 and 1990, litter on

Texas highways reduced by 72 percent. Why did it succeed? Because the "target customer"—men driving trucks on highways—felt a sense of state pride when they saw the signs. The campaign aligned littering with "messing" with their home state, with their own identity as Texans, and people stopped throwing trash out their car windows. It wasn't long before "Don't Mess with Texas" became a declaration of identity for all Texans. We are drawn to messaging that is *consistent* with our identity.

Identity is powerful. This is why intentional polarization can also be an effective attractor factor. We are drawn to messaging that affirms we are right and other people are wrong. Why do you think so many Democrats watch MSNBC and so many Republicans watch Fox News? Because they are attracted to that which affirms their thinking, their beliefs—all that makes them who they are—and they are repelled by that which goes against their identity.

Is the Timing Right for Your Marketing Idea?

After George Floyd was murdered and the nation was consumed by a racial reckoning, I put a stop to a Get Different Experiment. I had planned to have a hot air balloon flying low over a town with a sign that read EARTHLINGS. WE HAVE COME TO SAVE SMALL BUSINESS. READ PROFIT FIRST. It was meant to be a wildly different way to market a book and, I hoped, get on the news, but I felt it was now inappropriate. It was absolutely not the right time to market—to anyone.

A couple of weeks later, I read a post on Facebook that confirmed I had made the right decision. Dr. Venus Opal Reese, author of *Black Woman Millionaire: Hot Mess Edition,* had posted a screenshot of her unsubscribing from a mailing list that included her "reason why" message. It ended with "I can't hear your marketing. I am too busy trying to be sane, sober, safe, and alive." Along with the screenshot, Dr. Reese posted a message to all marketers. The opening line is important:

"I hereby evict you from my inbox. My email. My snail mail. If you don't care about me in the midst of all we are dealing with in this real-life/real-time moment, I don't want you in my inbox. You are not welcome here."

People know when they are being marketed to, and they know when you are taking advantage of a crisis. They also know when you *ignore* the crisis. So, be mindful of timing. Don't send marketing that might hurt someone or demonstrate a lack of empathy or understanding. Ask yourself, "Does this serve my ideal prospect?" And, "Is this the right time to send this message?" A different message may need to go out, one that speaks to the events of the day and how it may be affecting your community.

Will Your Gimmick Get You Where You Want to Go?

In 2019, I recruited a bunch of authors to meet up and share our best strategies for growing readership, and our brands. Don Miller, the author of *Building a StoryBrand* agreed to host the event at his beautiful Nashville home. Sitting among authors I admired—Don, Ryan Holiday (*The Daily Stoic*), James Clear (*Atomic Habits*), Jon Gordon (*The Energy Bus*), Chris Guillebeau (*The $100 Startup*), and John Ruhlin (*Giftology*)—I was pumped to drop my best marketing strategies. One of them involves selling your own books as used books on Amazon, and then surprising customers with a free upgrade. This approach creates buzz because buyers are psyched to get a fresh, clean copy and sometimes share that on social media. It clearly Differentiates, Attracts, and Directs. Or does it?

After delivering this book-marketing hack of the century, I anxiously awaited my standing ovation. Or at least minor applause. Or at least one cricket clapping. None of it happened.

Ryan Holiday stared straight ahead at the crackling fireplace. Then he said, "I hate this idea. It fuckin' sucks."

Ouch. That was a swift kick to the ego's nuts. My cheeks went hot. My throat went dry. I looked at Ryan as he continued to look at the fireplace.

"What do you mean, Ryan?" I said, trying to hold my defenses back.

That's when Ryan Holiday, the authority on stoicism and general smartness, started dropping logic bombs.

"You are thinking way too small, Mike. You are wowing people who don't see enough value in your book to get a new one. They are cheap buyers looking for cheap fixes. Why would you ever try to wow them?"

The room was silent. James Clear and Chris Guillebeau nodded in eyebrows-raised "um, yeah, that's obvious" agreement. I resisted the urge to slide down in my chair and instead fixed my eyes on Ryan's jean jacket, lined with sheep's wool. He looked like a cowboy.

"Worse," he continued, "your marketing is small. You've got to ask a bigger question. You want to sell millions of books, and this gimmick sells onesie-twosies."

Ryan stayed locked in on the fireplace for one more beat. Then, he turned to face me and said, again, "This idea really fuckin' sucks."

Ryan is a frighteningly smart, introspective, driven guy. He was the last guy to show up for our meeting and the first to leave. He doesn't waste time on niceties and bullshit. He's also about fifteen years younger than I am. I tried to get past all of that, but his advice went down hard.

On the flight home, I got real with myself. Ryan was right: I had focused on a marketing idea that only yielded onesie-twosies. And because that idea worked, I ignored the fact that it was only inching me along toward my goal.

To be clear, I do not agree with Ryan about my bargain buyers. If you bought this book on discount, or checked it out from your library, or found it in a box of free books on the street (that happened, by the way), it makes no difference to me. I'm all for saving as many bucks as you can, and I value each and every one of my readers.

And I don't agree with Ryan about "gimmicks." They get a bad rap. If a gimmick drives consistent, significant business, I'll use them all day long.

But he was right about one thing. I had been thinking too small. The discount marketing approach generated one or two book sales at a time, and stopped with the end reader. If I wanted to eradicate entrepreneurial poverty, I would need to move a lot more books. Millions of books.

I started asking myself, "How do I move one hundred more copies of my books each day?" That better question has yielded better answers. I used Get Different Experiments to evaluate and test ideas that will help me attract the type of readers (and groups) who will buy dozens, if not hundreds of books. I achieved it through multiple, different techniques. I set up a new email sequence. I modified my web properties. I changed up the format of virtual keynotes. And, most effectively, I added a level of marketing where people use my books to market themselves. As a result, I sold many more books, and those sales helped me increase my advance on *this* book by a significant multiple. This is not to brag, but this points to the critical power of different.

The advance I received for this book was hundreds of thousands *more* than what I sold my first company for. My first company took me eight years to build and sell. Radically improving my book sales took me eight minutes of listening and a few hours of Get Different Experiments.

A few months after our author meetup, I texted Ryan. "Hey, Ryan. Just wanted to thank you for what you shared. Your advice literally made me hundreds of thousands of dollars. Thank you so much, brother."

His response: "NP."

Classic Holiday.

As you evaluate whether or not your different idea is worth pursuing, be honest with yourself—as honest as Ryan was with me. Are you in love with an idea that seems awesome on the surface, but will end up appealing to prospects that can take you only so far? Are you thinking small? You may have to go back and revise your ideal avatar. That's okay, by the way. You don't have to get everything right on the first go-round. This is an experiment, remember?

~~~~~

While researching Geek Squad for this book, I came upon a 2012 interview Stephens did with Clay Collins.[14] I wrote this quote down: "Geek Squad had to stand out, because we couldn't afford to be in the Yellow pages, we couldn't afford to have billboards. . . . Everything [was] marketing because we had no money for marketing." *Everything was marketing because they had no money for marketing.* I like that. I'd heard Stephens say that the best thing that ever happened to him was not having any money to market his business, and now I understood why.

In that same interview, I read that Stephens viewed their marketing as "one large performance art experiment." Because I had been doing the Get Different Experiments for months, this was more confirmation that thinking about Get Different marketing as an experiment is the way to cut through the noise of self-judgment. They weren't afraid to try unconventional stuff to get attention. The Savannah Bananas do out-of-the-box stuff all the time. Me, I'm always doing weird stuff. Just make sure *your* different stuff, whatever it may be, acts like a beacon in the night for the people you want to serve.

Your Turn

Before you move on to the Direct stage, determine whether your different marketing idea will attract your ideal customer—and how you can make it *more* attractive to them. Remember, all three of the DAD elements work together and do *not* work on their own. So again, don't skip this exercise!

Step 1: Identify three Attraction Influencers that are consistent with how you want to market your prospects. Here's a list to get you started:

Authority

Beauty

Social significance

Consistency

Safety

Comfort

Expansion

Significance

Health

Relief

Belonging

Purpose

Curiosity

Trusted source

Repetition

Then for each of the three techniques you've selected, describe how you will use this technique in conjunction with your different idea to make it attractive.

Step 2: If you can, blend the three Attraction Influencers to amplify the impact. Or if they can't be blended in some capacity, pick the one that you believe is the most attractive to your ideal prospect. Write down or draw how you will use the attractor factor to engage the prospect. Write or draw how this will work with the different element you have selected.

Step 3: Determine whether your idea complies with Attract and, if it does, check that box on your Get Different Experiment sheet.

My Turn

I set up a shelving system that has my books positioned over my shoulder, based upon my Differentiate idea. Then I started playing with the Attract stage as I tested my idea.

Medium: All videos prerecorded and live broadcast.

Idea: An unignorable bookshelf displaying my books, which inspires people to get them.

Attract: Differentiate is checked off, but can be amplified. Working on something that keeps people's eyes on the bookshelf and the books on the shelf.

Back Side of Get Different Experiment Sheet: Looking at Attract, I used a standard bookshelf and placed my books prominently. I noticed when people watched live videos I was able to download the chat at the conclusion. People would have off-topic conversations, including about the bookshelf. It was clear that having the books over my right shoulder got more attention than my left. Perhaps this is the F pattern people follow when scanning a screen. What are ideas that are even more attractive than standard bookshelves? Searching Google and Etsy for "unique bookshelves."

I also found a bookcase that looked like a tree. A tree bookcase! This could be a play on the

Tree of Knowledge. That is consistent with my brand, to provide knowledge that simplifies the entrepreneurial journey. And the tree bookcase may keep people more engaged than a standard shelf. I found a builder on Etsy to make it. Cost is twelve hundred dollars. It is a onetime cost, and I present to more than two hundred fifty people a week on live video. My hypothesis is that within five weeks I am at my one-dollar-per-prospect investment, and over time that per prospect cost will drop to pennies.

The tree bookcase leverages the Attraction Influencers of curiosity and beauty.

I am improving my experiment parameters and will try with this potentially more attractive bookshelf. Just one more thing, I need to get the Direct approved first.

CHAPTER SIX

Direct for Results

L ove them or hate them, many street performers are marketing savants. They show up in a way that is different that gets noticed and attracts their ideal audience—most of the time. And, they have the Direct step down pat. When you walk by a pop-up opera singer, or a breakdancing troupe, or some guy with a guitar, you know exactly what they want you to do: put money in the bucket. They want you to show appreciation for their uniqueness by giving them a tip. They don't give you a sequence of things to do. You won't see a sign that reads:

1. Take a picture.

2. Post it to social media.

3. Add the description and the address of this street corner.

4. When you're done, please tip whatever amount you can afford.

And they don't give you a list of options:

- Follow me on Instagram and Twitter.

- Applaud dramatically. Be that overclapper everyone "loves."

- Do that stupid gaping-mouth, looking-around thing so other people notice.

Or:

- Sign up for my mailing list.

- Visit my website to book me for a private show.

- Leave me a fat tip.

The instructions are as clear as they are obvious. You know exactly what to do. Fill that damn bucket full of damn cash, now. The clarity and specificity on what to do does not guarantee the prospect will pay up, but it maximizes the odds that they will.

Adding steps and giving too many options creates friction, as author and neuromarketing pioneer Roger Dooley explains in his book of the same name. With every marketing offer, make sure you have one clear directive, and make it easy to do.

You can even make your directive more specific to get the exact result you want. Having a clear directive ensures you will get more responses, so more tips. What if you want those tips to be larger bills?

When my sons Jake and Tyler worked at Beignets doughnut shop in Denville, New Jersey, I told them, "Salt that tip jar with fives and tens. People will see those bills and tip more than they would have otherwise." It worked. Even if customers didn't drop a fiver in their jar, they *did* put in at least a couple of bucks, which was more than the average tip customers gave before they started this strategy. To customers who noticed the previous tips, fives and tens seemed to be "the norm," and they gave accordingly.

You can take things too far. Jake and Tyler could have salted that jar with a hundred-dollar bill, but at a certain point the ask becomes unreasonable. A customer who spots a one-hundred-dollar tip in the jar may be put off because they can't match that amount, or because they simply think it's an outrageous amount, and they may justify tipping nothing because someone already gave a hefty tip that covers the nongivers. When giving direction, be specific and be reasonable.

Cornell University's Center for Hospitality Research released a report[1] detailing twenty research-backed strategies servers can use to get more and better tips. You've probably received a restaurant bill that included recommended tipping percentages at the bottom, right? That's one way to get people to tip more, simply because it's *specific* and *easier* for them—they don't have to do the math. Most people appreciate this information and, as a result, tip more.

In another test, customers were given a card that suggested

specific percentages based on quality of service: 15 percent for "adequate" service, 20 percent "better-than-average service," or 25 percent for "outstanding service." This approach reduced the number of really high tips, so that the average number of tips over the course of a day remained the same, or sometimes even resulted in a lower total. This was as a result of two obvious problems with that approach. First is the friction of having to think about which category your dining experience fit into *before* you leave your tip. Second is the "adequate" category. Most people are reluctant to give high marks for service unless it is truly spectacular, so if you are a person who routinely gives 20 percent, following the "quality of service" guidelines may cause you to actually give a lower tip—15 percent—than you normally would.

Giving diners guidance about how much people *normally* tip resulted in the highest increases in tip amounts. Not just doing the math, but doing the math *and* showing how most people tip at that restaurant. It's like setting out a tip bucket and seeding it with fives and tens.

The final step in the DAD Marketing Framework is to ensure that your Get Different marketing has a singular directive—one simple, doable call to action. Get those "fives and tens!"

Your Directive Can Be Simple

If you've ever been to the Badlands, you've seen the signs for Wall Drug. In fact, their hand-painted billboards can be seen for more than six hundred miles of Interstate 90, from Minnesota to Montana. It was those signs, as famous as the store itself, that helped Ted and Dorothy Hustead save their fledgling drugstore in the "middle of nowhere"—Wall, South Dakota. The locals had been hit hard by the Great Depression, and shortly after they bought the store in 1931, they realized they did not have enough customers. Still, Dorothy was optimistic they would succeed, and they agreed to give it five years.

Just months before their five-year deadline, and still struggling to get customers in the store, Dorothy came up with an idea inspired by the incessant sound of the "cars going by on Route 16A." She thought about the travelers' long drive across the prairie and figured they would probably want some ice-cold water. The Husteads had plenty of both ice and water, and she thought if they offered it for free to people driving by, they could get those people to come into the store. Once inside, those travelers would become customers and buy other things.

The directive was simple: Come to Wall Drug for free ice water. To get drivers' attention, Dorothy borrowed (remember R & D?) an idea from Burma-Shave. By the time she got her idea, the shaving cream company had been printing slogans on small, sequential signs and placing them on highways all over the US for more than a decade. Each sign had a piece of the phrase. Some were about their product:

Shaving brushes / Soon you'll see 'em / On the shelves / Of some museum / Burma-Shave

And some were about traffic safety:

Don't take a curve / at 60 per. / We hate to lose / a customer / Burma-Shave

The signs were very effective in getting travelers to keep paying attention to the signs to get the full message. It was a classic play on the attraction of curiosity. Keep the prospect engaged by giving them something incomplete, occupying their mind during the ho-hum drive down the highway until they passed the next sign to see if they were right in their guess. Burma-Shave occupied the minds of prospects for many a minute of their drive. That is damn good marketing, and Dorothy knew it. So she came up with her own poem for their signs:

Get a soda / Get a root beer / turn next corner / just as near / to Highway 16 & 14 / Free Ice Water / Wall Drug

Ted and their son painted the signs on twelve-by-thirty-six-inch boards and put them along the highway. By the time they got back to the store, customers had already shown up. Dorothy's idea worked—the signs were different enough to attract their ideal customers, and the directive told them exactly what to do. Did you get that? They had customers showing up before the marketers, Dorothy's crew, got back to the shop. Different works. And sometimes it works stupid fast.

By the next summer, the Husteads had to hire eight sales clerks to help them handle all of their customers. Eventually, Wall Drug expanded and became a major tourist stop, attracting millions of visitors every summer. They added a gift shop and other stores, restaurants, an art museum, and an eighty-foot brontosaurus sculpture (*cough*—different—*cough*). They are still family-owned and they still offer free ice water, but now they also give free bumper stickers, and let their customers do the marketing for them.

Robert Stephens, our Geek Squad pal, once said in a classroom lecture, "I would argue the more boring a business is, the greater the opportunity there is to differentiate." Boring offers massive opportunity, because the definition of boring is sameness. Computer guys are boring, pizza delivery is boring, drugstores are extremely boring (hence one reason people seek drugs). If your industry is boring, go do a happy dance right now, because with an itty-bitty piece of Get Different magic you will stand out. A boring drugstore became unboring enough to millions of people with the differentiation factor of a sequential poem promising free ice water. Oh my word! How easy it is to get noticed! And once you do, to send millions of people your way!

Your singular call to action can be as simple as "come get some free ice water." In fact, the simpler the better. You could keep it so simple, you don't even need words. To get more people to use the stairs rather than the adjacent escalator, the city of Brussels made the stairs musical. They painted them to look like black-and-white piano keys and rigged each step to play a different note each time someone stepped on them. No signs urging people to choose the stairs. No messages about health or exercise. Just a set of painted, musical stairs that got noticed, and engaged people who wanted to have fun, compelling them to take the stairs. The DAD was built right in. Musical steps are noticeable (different), fun (attractive), and actionable (directive), all without saying a word.

When Your Marketing Triggers the Wrong Action—or No Action

Have you heard of *The Sims*? *Madden NFL*? If not, just know that these are wildly successful video games, produced by

Electronic Arts (EA). In 2009, the company launched the *Godfather II* video game with a different marketing idea. Hoping to get the press to talk up the game, EA sent game reviewers and other media influencers brass knuckles. The problem? Someone on that team didn't do their homework and assess the risk, and it was a doozy. Brass knuckles are illegal to own, without a concealed weapon permit, in many states, so not only did EA send a weapon through the mail, in almost all the cases, they sent an *illegal* weapon in the mail.

In the end, EA had to request that the media influencers return the brass knuckles. While EA did end up generating media buzz around the *Godfather II* game, ultimately it wasn't about the game at all—it was about the brass knuckle fiasco. Their different marketing was noticeable for sure; it caught attention. It was "attractive" to some folks, too. I mean, how many times have you seen brass knuckles in person, let alone received them in the mail? Curiosity kept people's attention: "Did you get a pair of brass knuckles yet?" But the marketing campaign fell apart at the last step. It triggered action for sure, but it triggered the wrong action. EA didn't Direct, it distracted.

Big companies get it wrong all the time, but the return consistently outweighs the risk. It is much more likely you have heard of *The Sims* and *Madden* but probably didn't know the brass knuckles story—or the *Godfather II* video game, for that matter. When different fails, in most cases, it disappears into the ether. Trying something different is worth it, but do heed the warning of common sense. Because, sometimes, just sometimes, a company takes a risk without any consideration for the consequence. It just goes with its big stupid idea.

Take the marketing campaign for the animated TV show *Aqua Teen Hunger Force*. In 2007, Turner Broadcasting placed a bunch of blue glowing and blinking devices in random public locations in New York, Boston, and eight other major metropolitan areas. I'm going to give you just a moment to think about why that might not have worked out. A glowing and blinking device. In New York. In Boston. Under bridges, in tunnels, at subway entrances. How do you think that worked for them?

Yup, you're right. It played out like a bad sitcom. City residents assumed the devices were bombs, and notified the police, and suddenly this clever marketing idea became a terrorism scare that ended up shutting down roadways and had local and federal law enforcement searching for bombs all over the city. Turner Broadcasting had hoped people and the media would talk up the show. Instead, they labeled the marketing campaign a hoax. Well, not everyone. Just the governor of Massachusetts. Everyone else was just super pissed and used language that even a guy like me from Jersey won't say. Yeah, it was that bad.

Sometimes, a marketing idea doesn't trigger any action at all. I call this the "Hook, line, and stinker." You had a great attention grabber, your people were interested, and then—poof. Nothing for them to do, except maybe say, "That was cool." Like that time I asked book launch "Buzz Warriors" to stand in a public space and read aloud from *The Pumpkin Plan,* in an Old English accent, no less. Yeah. That was unconventional and got some attention, but it didn't lead to any book sales. Or new subscribers to my email list. The idea didn't work because I forgot to Direct people to do *anything.*

We see this all of the time with web design. You visit a website and have no clue about next steps. Sometimes, you don't even know what it is you're supposed to buy. Or the ubiquitous "Learn More" button is all over the site, when the primary idea for a website is to friggin' learn more in the first place.

In his awesome book about web design, *Don't Make Me Think*, Steve Krug says visitors don't consume, they scan. In a way, the world is a web page, and we are constantly scanning, looking for what is different, if it's for us, and if there is a clear action to take. Can your ideal customer easily figure out your singular call to action, or is it a mystery they have to solve? The next, singular step better be extremely obvious and extremely clear. If you get cute or you overwhelm them with choice, you simply confuse them. And as my good friend Don Miller, author of *Marketing Made Simple,* says, "If you confuse, you lose."

The confusion may not always be obvious to you. So your good buddies, Mr. Metrics and Ms. Measurements, will help you here. Match that up with active listening, and simple calls to action will become more and more apparent.

When signing books after speaking, I would open to the first blank page, add the guest's name, and then sign my name. Time permitting, I would add a generic message such as, "You've got this!" Or, "You rock!" Then one day at one event, I noticed a woman in line watching me sign. Typically, people chat with each other, or try to catch the conversation I'm having with whoever is in front of me. Not this woman. She focused her eagle eyes on the signature, on *how I did it*.

When it was her turn, she slid her copy of *Profit First* across the table and said, "You're signing the book on the wrong page.

Sign the title page so when people post on social media, the title is there."

At first, my fat ego took over and I thought, "*Who the hell are you?* I'm an amazing, super-important, special author guy (ahem, according to my mom). People are here to see special ol' me! I know how to sign a damn book, because, you know, I'm special. Mom says!"

Then, after I climbed over my King Kong–size ego-driven hissy fit, I said, "You know, that's a great point. Thank you."

Duh. I'd been signing books in a way that, even if readers *did* post their autograph page on social media, did not actually help me raise awareness for my books—because it was a blank page! Still, what difference would it make if not many people actually posted their pics?

Another duh: while I knew that people respond to seeing or hearing their own name, I had forgotten the importance of the personal message. Even though it requires a bit more time— thirty to sixty seconds, tops—I thought it would be more efficient to go with general messages. Plus, I'm not that creative after I've signed a couple of dozen books. The thing is, though, a personal message plays into readers' esteem. (Remember, Esteem is one of the Attraction Influencers.) And, when they see their name plus a personal message, they are much more likely to take a picture of that autograph and post it for all the world to see.

Ever since, I've signed my books differently. I make sure to sign on the title page and include the reader's name and a personal message. As a result, when people share the autograph page on their social, their followers now see the title of my book. I also include a little business card that reads "Send me a picture of you holding the book open to the signature page so I can send you a thank-you gift of bonus content for the book." They send me the picture, which is a specific, reasonable ask, and I send them bonus content with the next reasonable ask: to post the picture on social media. Coupled with the card's specific directive, about half the readers for which I sign books post a picture on social media. Once I followed all the parts of DAD, I went from zilch to zillions. You can, too.

Some Direct fails cannot be fixed. Yeah, I'm looking at you, brass knuckle and blinking-bomb geniuses. And some fails can be fixed by making small tweaks, like my dummy move with blank-page autographs. To avoid the big fat fails entirely, think your experiment through. Will the directive trigger the wrong action? Or no action at all? You won't be able to predict every outcome, no one can, but you can avoid the major gaffes with a little thought time.

Design Your Directive for Your Community

Did you know that bees see colors on the ultraviolet light spectrum? This means that they see many more variations than humans do. Because they can see more colors, bees and other insects can spot the differences in parts of a flower that, to us, look like one color. This helps them land on flowers and find the stamens and pistils. So ask yourself, what can your community see, hear, or understand that other people can't? What would they respond to that other people might not?

Dorothy Hustead of Wall Drug understood her ideal customers very well. She knew they had traveled a long way over a seemingly endless prairie. She also knew they were likely hot and thirsty. So, she came up with a directive that would appeal to them: free ice-cold water. For the best results, design your directive for your community. What would appeal to them specifically?

Identity also plays a role in getting people to take action. Think about how your directive may confirm your ideal customers' sense of self. This is why language is so important. Understanding the lingo of your ideal customer can make or break your directive.* The video game store GameStop fell into the break category.

GameStop created an ad designed to get millennials to buy a bundle of games. The directive was to vote on which bundle they should offer at a premium. The problem was, the language turned off millennials—big-time. The ad read: "GameStop be like which bundle do you want for $7.50?" They became the butt of a joke among the customers they wanted to attract because they said something a millennial would not say. As a result, their marketing idea flopped. If you plan to speak your customers' language, it better be a language you speak. The language has to be appropriate for both audience and context.

In *Switch: How to Change Things When Change Is Hard*, authors Chip and Dan Heath explain the challenge of conflicting motivation through an analogy of an elephant and a rider. The

---

* Check out *Lingo: Discover Your Ideal Customer's Secret Language and Make Your Business Irresistible*, by Jeffrey Shaw, to master the language of your community.

rider is the logical, rational part of the brain, while the elephant is the emotional, impulsive part of the brain. The rider may say, "I need to lose ten pounds." The elephant may say, "I want to eat chocolate chip cookies." The elephant is bigger and stronger than the rider, so it wins against the logic.

To influence your prospect to take the action you want, you must align the rider and the elephant so they both want the same thing, your Direct. The solution? An appeal that aligns with both emotion and logic. When you use the Direct, ask yourself what serves the instant gratification of your customers' emotional desire (quick wins, easy steps, fast rewards), and satisfies the long-term logical desires (permanent change, noticeable impact and improvement). If you sell grills, for example, the instant benefit may be a free "what to watch out for when firing up your grill" report. Long-term satisfaction? A lifelong, worry-free grilling experience.

The Three Motivators

The way you Direct a community depends entirely on your relationship with them. Do they see you as

1. someone superior,

2. someone equal, or

3. someone inferior?

In other words, do they aspire to be like you, gain from you, or learn from you—a superior position where you can give advice or assistance? Or do they see you as one of them, as an equal who can commune, share, and exchange? Or do they see you as inferior, in a position where you can gain from them?

Relationship positioning depends on the circumstances around the moment. For example, members of a church experience all three types of relationships in a service. During a sermon, the church is in a position of superiority. During the offering, the church is in a position of inferiority. And during the post-service coffee gathering, the church is typically in a position of equality.

As a provider of goods and services to your client, you will experience all three relationship positions. The question is, with what you are marketing now, how does the prospect see the relationship in that moment? Bias and ignorance are factors here, so you might not be sure how your prospects perceive you; experiment and test until you figure it out.

If you are in a superior position, *tell* them the action to take. "Buy this shirt" or "learn from me" would be examples of a directive in the superior context. Commanding verbs are the strongest action statement when you are perceived as the authority in the relationship. Reward their compliance to your request with demonstrations of relational advancement. Phrases such as "you have made a great decision" and "you will love this shirt" and "way to step up."

If you are seen as an equal, then *invite* them to "join our community" or "connect with us." Inclusive verbs are the strongest action statements for equal relationships. Reward compliance to your request by showing your prospect's significance in the community. Notify your community with messages such as "we would like everyone to welcome our newest member" or "[Customer's Name] is part of the family."

And if you are in the inferior position, where your community feels that you will gain from their knowledge, resources, or abilities, *petition* them to take action with messages such as "share your experience" or "tell us how to serve you" or "contribute now!" Appeal verbs are the strongest action statements when you are perceived as the primary benefactor of the exchange. Reward compliance with your request by acknowledging their superior position. For example, "you have made a big difference" or "thank you for leading the way" or "your generosity will not be forgotten."

Many motivational speakers are in a position superior to their fans.* So, if they try to use inferior position language, such as "tell me what I can do for you," it's not going to work well. But if their direction is "attend my five-day training," then they win. Conversely, if a mastermind association such as Entrepreneurs' Organization (EO) says, "Attend our five-day training," the message won't be as successful as it would be if EO said, "Join your entrepreneurial peers," or, "Apply to become a member." And if you are Kiva, an organization that serves poor populations by facilitating microloans to business owners, saying, "Apply to contribute" won't be as effective as "serve business owners

---

* Visit gogetdifferent.com and get the free resources to see an example of how I did a Get Different strategy with my "relationship" with celebrities. I think you will find it, you know, different.

who need you" or "elevate others." Direction must fit position or it falls flat.

Pour Fuel on the Action

At Newark Airport's Terminal C, you can dine at a restaurant called Classified. That is, if you know it exists. And where it is. And if you have an invitation or reservation. To get access to this stellar restaurant, in fact, to even know it exists, you have to be a 1K member of United Airlines' frequent-flier program, or know someone who is, *and* get invited. When I finally got on the Classified member list, I made sure to allow time to eat there on my very next business trip. Why? Because just knowing about it made me feel special. Being allowed in made me feel like a big shot. And because I *love* feeling like a big shot, I don't keep the secret. I tell *everyone* about the restaurant. In fact, I sent a crew of ten friends there just so I could "get them in." Whenever I travel with my family, we go to Classified. Why? Because we can. I know the marketing "trick," yet my "it feels good to be special and feel like a big shot" ego keeps me going and keeps me opening my wallet.

Secrets can trigger extreme loyalty. Knowing about a secret, exclusive restaurant in Newark Airport is a significant reason why I am a loyal United customer. Most airlines are good at secrets, exclusivity, and scarcity. They all have silver, gold, platinum, diamond, whatever—semiprecious metal or plastic gems— statuses that make their customers feel special and important.

Once a flier reaches an "elite" status, they are not likely to fly another airline. That's the power of, you know, bigwig status.

Ajito is a Japanese restaurant in Calgary that is hidden behind an old-fashioned Coca-Cola machine. Literally, that's their front door. You could walk right by and never know about it. How is it a marketing win? Because people love a secret, underground place. They like that challenge of "discovering" secret places and the allure of being "in the know."

In Towaco, New Jersey, the restaurant Rails has two bars: one is off the main dining room and the other is a secret bar, hidden behind a bookshelf. (See? I really can't be trusted with secrets. Don't tell me *anything*. Except tell me *everything*.) Any guesses which bar is the most crowded?

And if you really want to ramp up the power of Direct, limit its availability. As I mentioned earlier, I'm in the market for a pickup truck. When I started my search in 2020, the new Ford Bronco was made available for order, with ship dates starting in 2021. There are seven different versions you can choose from. There is unlimited supply if you are simply willing to wait for it to arrive, and demand is robust. One model is very limited, the First Edition, which is more than twice as expensive as the basic model. Yet it sold out within minutes. Twice! The First Edition Ford Bronco's allocated thirty-five hundred units sold out so fast that Ford responded by doubling the production run to seven thousand to accommodate the "I missed out by minutes" complaints that poured in from people waiting but not able to click-clack and type in their credit card info fast enough. Ford doubled the availability and minutes later hit capacity again.

When something is scarce, it can pour fuel on the action. I

wasn't even looking for a Bronco, and I couldn't click "Build Your Bronco" fast enough, because if I waited, I would miss out on my First Edition shot. I didn't buy the Bronco, never even seriously considered it, but under the power of scarcity, I took way more steps than I expected. I strongly suspect I would have plopped down a deposit if I could have. Probably while stuffing my face with chocolate chip cookies (damn elephant).

As a side note, I analyzed my internet search time for a new car, and ever since the Bronco First Edition urgency, I noticed that I spent 68 percent more time looking at Ford products than all the other car manufacturers combined. That is the other power of scarcity: when you don't make it into the scant supply and miss out, some of us will at least want to stay in the club. No Bronco, but I did put down a deposit on a new, pure electric car from Ford coming out in 2022. And no, I wasn't in the market for that, either.

~~~~

You know you need a singular, very specific directive to ensure your marketing efforts get results, but what should it be? To figure this out, simply ask yourself, "What exactly do I want my ideal prospects to do at this stage?" Click and buy. Subscribe to a list or follow on social. Those are easy, clear asks. Sometimes, though, you need your customer to follow multiple steps or paths to get the results you want.

So start with the end in mind and work your way backwards. You already did this by setting the Objective parameters of Who,

What, and Win. You know the ideal prospect (Who), which offer serves them best (What), and the ultimate outcome you want (Win). Knowing the Win, reverse engineer the fewest steps that are digestible for the prospect that get you to that Win. Each action in a sequence of steps you want your prospects to take must meet these two qualifiers: (1) it is a reasonable ask (not too much too soon, and not too little too late), and (2) it is a safe ask (where the potential reward outweighs the perceived risk for the prospect).

Once you've settled on a clear directive, make sure *all* of your ideal prospects can take that action. For example, does your ask require people to have a specific type of phone? Or to use a specific web browser? Or to pay only in cash? How can you ensure that your call to action is doable—virtually effortless—for most (ideally all) of your desired prospects? You may not prepare for every contingency, so be prepared to get feedback during your experiments and subsequent rollouts. Listen to prospects who point out where it is confusing or hard for them.

Remember, more options cause confusion, so identify *one* call to action that is accessible for almost all of your target audience. In his book *The Paradox of Choice*, psychologist Barry Schwartz explained that too much choice can lead to paralysis. You know that feeling when you're staring at a twenty-page diner menu full of options and you can't decide what to order? The paradox of choice is like that, and you want to avoid making your ideal customers feel that way. Give them *one* and *only one* action to take.

Refine your directive further by informing people what to expect when they take that action. What will happen when they go to the web page, or call the phone number, or sign up for your awesome thing?

Your Turn

You're at the final stage of the DAD Marketing Framework, so let's take this baby home. Remember, effective marketing requires a specific directive. What's yours?

> **Step 1:** Review or refine the ultimate action you want your prospect to take, the final purchase objective. You already documented this as the WIN in the first step of your Get Different Experiment Sheet.
>
> **Step 2:** Then, note the immediate action you want them to take at this stage.
>
> **Step 3:** Finally, write the phrase (or positioning) you will use to Direct your prospect to take this immediate action. Confirm that this phrase or whatever form of directive you create is clear, specific, reasonable, and actionable. If it is, check that box on the Get Different Experiment sheet.

My Turn

Past testing proved out that the unique positioning of books on my traditional bookshelf worked in getting attention (Differentiate) and moderate engagement (Attract). With my new test of the tree bookcase, I want to get stronger attention (Differentiate) and keep people locked in longer (Attract), and I also need to ensure I nailed the Direct phase with a specific and reasonable ask.

I refine the Direct idea to get to my best guest before I test. I do this, as you should, on the back of my piece of paper.

> <u>Medium</u>: All videos prerecorded and live broadcast.
>
> <u>Idea</u>: An unignorable tree-shaped bookcase displaying my books, which inspires people to get them.
>
> <u>DAD Approved?</u> Yes to Differentiate with a tree bookcase, although only testing will prove it works. Yes to Attract with a tree bookcase because the structure will make our eyes naturally wander around. . . . Testing will be needed to prove, of course. Now time to do the Direct (on the back of the sheet).
>
> <u>Direct</u>: I present to more than two hundred fifty people a week. I can put a sign up that reads, get these books on Amazon, but that

almost feels too salesy. Like a retail window. Because I am the one presenting, what if I say something like this: "You may have noticed the books over my shoulder. I wrote them to simplify the entrepreneurial journey. If you feel that may serve you, please go to Amazon right now to get a copy."

I can also reward people by posting in the chat which book they just ordered, and send them free bonus content as a thank-you. That will also have a social proof mechanism; when people see others doing a behavior, they will replicate it. This is a strong clear Direct.

I have improved all my experiment parameters and feel I have maximized my likelihood of success. Now I am ready to run the test!

~~~~~~~~~~~~~~~~~~~~~~~~~

CHAPTER SEVEN

Experiment, Measure, Amplify, Repeat

L et's just get this out of the way right now: Some of your different ideas will suck. Scratch that. *Most* of your different ideas will suck. I would venture to guess that more than 90 percent of my own different ideas were bummers—they failed in the marketing milliseconds. But the 10 percent that *did* go the distance, they more than made up for the experiments that didn't.

When Michelle Scribner, the CEO of Sum of All Numbers, read an early version of this book, she threw it against the wall in her hotel room. She was pissed that it could take nine tries to get one good idea. She was pissed because she knows it's the truth. You may be pissed by the failure rate, too. But I will not waste your time with comfortable lies. This is the hard truth. You must be different, and you need to find that different through trial, trial, and trial again.

Through the process of flopping, you'll generate spectacular winners, for sure. This trickle of winners in a sea of losers may make you want to give up. You may start to wonder if any of your ideas will work. Or you may feel as if some ideas are just too risky to try. When you feel that way, remember that your competition feels this, too. Everyone experiences this magnetic pull back to what we have always done, the way everyone else does it. Not because it works, but because it feels safe.

So if you feel the pull to resort to the same fill-in-the-blank marketing method that everyone else is doing, don't worry. That's normal. If you hear coaches, agencies, and experts saying, "You need to do ___" where the blank is the marketing method that everyone else is saying, that's normal. But just because it's "normal" doesn't mean you should do it. Sure, you'll feel the pull to do it, but you absolutely shouldn't.

Doing different feels scary precisely because no one else is doing it—and that's why you must do it! Because no one else is doing it, that's precisely why it will be effective.

The inclination of us mere mortals is to blend in, so you may dismiss your ideas out of hand, without really considering whether or not they are actually worth pursuing. The human tendency to rein ourselves in kills invention and innovation, so I want you to get into the mindset that your ideas do not have to become permanent parts of your business marketing plan. They are simply experiments.

During my sixth-grade science class, when a cloud of smoke plumed out from mixing the wrong chemicals, Mr. Fordyce would say, "Good job, you just found something that might kill you. Let's not do that on a large scale. Let's try a new experiment." In the same way, you have a marketing hypothesis—this may work, this may not work—and you're going to run a test to figure out if you're onto something. No pressure to go big. No pressure to nail it out of the gate. No pressure to be perfect, or even close to perfect. Just fun lab experiments.

One of the reasons we buy courses and advertising packages is because we believe the stats vendors tout: email open rates, click-through rates, and percentages of engagement. We think because other businesses in our industry may be getting those returns on their investment, we will, too. So we put on our nicest gray suit and hope for the best as we step in line with the other gray suits. And this is when it happens. This is when we hear the greatest marketing lie of all time: if your marketing isn't working, you simply haven't done enough yet.

Yes, I mentioned that earlier—probably more than once. I repeat it because it's one of the most common sins marketing "experts" commit. Let it stink in. Yeah, I said "stink in." That's how rotten that lie is. I'll state it one more time for dramatic effect.

The number one marketing lie in the world:

If your marketing isn't working, you simply haven't done enough yet.

Ads not working? You need to do more. Website isn't converting? You need more traffic. Radio spot a flop? You need to put it on more stations, more times per day.

Remember Linda Weathers? She blew fifty grand trying to get just one lead, in part because she heard the message that she just wasn't doing enough volume. More, more, more.

All bullshit!

Pure, unadulterated bullshit.

If you are doing something and it's not working, it's likely not working because it is missing a component of the DAD. There's no question you have to achieve statistical significance (enough attempts that at least one person is highly likely to engage), but doing more of the same unnoticeable, ineffective stuff is a huge mistake. This is like saying no one can see the invisible man, so let's put the entire invisi-family up onstage. Now can you see them? Of course not. More invisible is still invisible.

On the flip side, we hesitate to try fresh ideas because there are no stats out there saying they will work. We don't know if people will get what we're trying to do, and if they *do* get it, we aren't sure if it will actually generate leads. If you thought about it for a few minutes, I'm sure you'd realize that you've had ideas in the past that you let die simply because you thought they were too risky to implement. Perhaps you thought your ideas would take too much time, too much money, or too much effort. In other words, they seemed too risky to try, so you put them on the back burner.

Have you ever thought about that phrase "put it on the back burner"? We think it means we are temporarily putting something on low heat to cook something else, planning to get back to it later. All that really happens is we end up forgetting about it entirely. And you know what happens when you forget something cooking on the stove—you ruin it, destroy the pan, and end up with some crusted-up thing that no one can ever consume.

We need to break down our marketing ideas from grand "marketing plans" to doable "marketing experiments." It's these little tests where we discover what works and what doesn't, and perhaps as important, we start to build our marketing muscle. This is where we figure out if we've mastered the milliseconds, if our ideas are worth rolling out on a big scale. Always start with marketing experiments (manageable and revealing) and then, with the successful ones, move on to marketing plans (comprehensive and continuous).

Some ideas, though, are not worth the time and money it would take to run the experiment. Therefore, I evaluate my ideas first, then experiment. I want you to do the same. Nothing will kill your confidence faster than a pile of failed attempts and a dwindling pile of cash, so first vet the idea and then conduct the experiment. In other words, do what you can to experiment cheaply. If the experiment is a success, or will be with a little tweaking, then invest more in it, roll it out, and watch your leads flood in.

But how do you figure out which ideas have potential and which ideas shouldn't see the light of day? You evaluate them to see if they adhere to the DAD and you track them to see if they actually work. In this chapter, I'll walk you through how to conduct your own Get Different Experiment. You've already completed most of the work involved. The next step is to take your idea for a spin and determine whether it's ready for rollout.

The Get Different Experiment Sheet

Have you ever met someone who comes up with tons of ideas? Great ones, fun ones, wacky ones, wickedly smart ones, just tons? How do they do it? It isn't that they have a special talent per se. They have a process. They may do it so fluidly that it is subconscious. Nonetheless, they have a process. The Get Different Experiment Sheet is a simple way to create actionable marketing ideas—your experiments. This is how you evaluate whether your marketing approach targets the right prospect with the right offer, leverages the DAD (Differentiate, Attract, Direct), *and* is worth pursuing.

I developed the Get Different Experiment Sheet for myself in rough form over a decade ago. I have tested it repeatedly on my own ideas, and with clients on their ideas. I use it so often that it has become automatic; I see different marketing opportunities everywhere. You have been working with this puppy throughout the book, ever since Chapter 3. We are going through it step-by-step so that it will be a no-brainer for you to use from this point forward.

As a reminder, you can get your free Get Different Experiment Sheet along with all the resources for this book at gogetdifferent .com. I recommend you print out spare sheets to have on hand as you continue to read this book. And if you really don't like worksheets, you can eyeball it here and follow along in your own notebook.

Before we complete the entire sheet, it's important that you try one experiment at a time. Ultimately you will brainstorm many

GD EXPERIMENT SHEET

FOR _____

DATE _____ TEST # _____

STEP 1: OBJECTIVE

WHO
Who is the ideal prospect?

_____

WHAT
What offer serves them best?

_____

WIN
What is the outcome you want?

STEP 2: INVESTMENT

CUSTOMER LTV:_____

The typical life-time value (revenue) of a customer.

CLOSE RATE ODDS: _____ OF EVERY _____

Your expected close rate of engaged prospects e.g. 1 of every 5.

INVESTMENT PER PROSPECT:_____

The dollar amount you are willing to risk to land a prospect.

NOTES:

STEP 3: EXPERIMENT

MEDIUM: _____

What marketing platform you will use? e.g. website, email, direct mail, billboard, etc.

IDEA:

DOES THIS COMPLY WITH THE DAD FRAMEWORK?

❏ **DIFFERENTIATE**
Is it unignorable?

❏ **ATTRACT**
Is it a safe opportunity?

❏ **DIRECT**
Is it a specific and reasonable ask?

STEP 4: MEASUREMENT

INTENTIONS	OUTCOMES
START DATE: _____	**END DATE:** _____
INTENDED # OF PROSPECTS: _____	**ACTUAL # OF PROSPECTS:**_____
INTENDED RETURN:_____	**ACTUAL RETURN:** _____
INTENDED INVESTMENT:_____	**ACTUAL INVESTMENT:** _____

OBSERVATIONS:

VERDICT {

EXPAND & TRACK	**RE-TEST**	**IMPROVE**	**ABANDON**
Use as ongoing strategy	Test new sample	Fix and retry	Start new experiment

The Get Different Experiment Sheet

ideas, but we will start with just one test. Trying to manage and track multiple, different marketing strategies will dilute your focus and drive you nuts. Plus, like cooking your favorite recipe, over time you may find that an extra dash of salt or a little less flour makes all the difference. A Get Different Experiment isn't a do or die. It is a do, redo, tweak, or die.

The good news is, if you have been following along, you've already completed steps one, two, and three. But to make sure we nail *everything*, I will go through all the elements again.

At the top of the Get Different Experiment Sheet, or a piece of paper, write your company name (in the FOR field), the date (in the DATE field), and the number of your experiment (in the TEST field). You're just getting started, so the number is one. I realize this is as basic as putting your name on top of your fifth-grade test, but there is a reason beyond simple organization. By putting a name on it, you take ownership. It's the first step in gaining the control I mentioned at the start of this chapter—control over business growth. When I put "FOR: The Michalowicz brand," or one of my company names at the top, I get this fire of a feeling I can only describe as a "let's do this" sensation. This isn't just some rando experiment; I'm not trying to get a good grade in science class. This is an experiment that could change my business forever. Soon, you'll have a whole stack of these puppies, and the number will help you find your (possibly, hopefully) brilliant different marketing idea. It's your own catalog of marketing genius.

Step 1: OBJECTIVE

If you completed the Take Action section at the end of Chapter 3, filling out this section will be a breeze. Basically, copy and paste! Note the following:

WHO—Who is your ideal prospect (or avatar, if you prefer that term)? Hopefully, you figured this out in Chapter 3. If not, no time like the present. Recall that an avatar is a set of qualities of the person you most want to work with. Note that I said "person," not group of people. Avoid general markets such as "all pilots" or "moms with small children" or "small children with moms" for that matter. Get nitty-gritty specific, such as "a pilot who is retiring this year and wants to start a new career" or "the mom with five kids under ten at home, who has not actually gone insane yet." (That last one is purely hypothetical, of course.) The more specific the avatar, the more powerful our different marketing becomes for these people. Knowing who they are in detail empowers you to make a very specific marketing approach.

WHAT—What offer serves your prospect best? Of your products and or services, which one would rock their world? What big promise does that product or service deliver?

WIN—What is the ultimate outcome you want? Do you want to sell your prospects something? Do you want them making a contribution, becoming a member, signing up for a class? The WIN is the endgame for your marketing. When we get to the DIRECT phase in step two, that is the immediate action you want them to take to get to the WIN. In some cases the DIRECT and the WIN are the same thing, like "buy the shirt," and in other cases you will use the DIRECT to get closer to the WIN, like "sign up to be notified when the shirt releases." Remember, the WIN is the ultimate outcome that *you* want. The DIRECT is the next step in getting there.

STEP 1: OBJECTIVE—The first stage of a Get Different Experiment, where the prospect, offer, and desired outcome are defined.

Step 2: INVESTMENT

Again, you may have already done this work in Chapter 3. In which case, you have a head start.

CUSTOMER LTV—What is the lifetime value of your customer? How much revenue could you earn over the course of your relationship with them?

CLOSE RATE ODDS—If you put forth your best effort, what are the chances you will land this customer? This is a simple x of every y statement.

INVESTMENT PER PROSPECT—Knowing your odds, how much are you willing to invest per marketing attempt to each individual prospect to get one of them to become a customer?

STEP 2: INVESTMENT

CUSTOMER LTV:_____

The typical lifetime value (revenue) of a customer.

CLOSE RATE ODDS:_____ **OF EVERY** _____

Your expected close rate of engaged prospects *e.g. 1 of every 5.*

INVESTMENT PER PROSPECT:_____

The dollar amount you are willing to risk to land a prospect.

NOTES:

STEP 2: INVESTMENT—The second stage of a Get Different Experiment, where the customer's LTV and associated per-prospect marketing investment are determined.

Step 3: EXPERIMENT

Next, work the DAD Marketing Framework. Building on everything you've learned, note the following:

MEDIUM—Which marketing platform will you use? If you use the same one as the rest of the industry, you will need to Differentiate enough that the common (ignorable) medium is irrelevant. Alternatively, use a different medium from your competition, and with this inherent differentiation, you have already upped your odds of getting noticed.

IDEA—Looking at the brainstorm list you came up with in Chapter 4, which marketing idea do you plan to test?

Then, ask yourself, "Does DAD approve?"

DIFFERENTIATE—Is your idea unignorable?

ATTRACT—Is it a safe opportunity?

DIRECT—Is it a specific and reasonable ask?

Check the boxes that apply. If you're able to tick off all three, you're good to try the experiment. If you aren't convinced that you can check the boxes, reform your idea until you can. You won't have proof DAD works until you experiment, but we first need to pass the test of your own instinct.

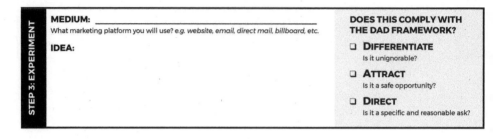

STEP 3: EXPERIMENT—The third stage of a Get Different Experiment, when the different marketing concept is proposed and evaluated for compliance with the DAD Marketing Framework.

Step 4: MEASUREMENT

If you're reasonably sure that your approach will get noticed, engage your ideal customer, and get them to take a specific action, then you're ready to test your theory. The truth is not said through words, but through action. Your prospects will "speak" the truth through their behavior. If you've read any of my other books or heard me speak, you probably know I'm a tester. I *love* a good test, because what's the point of spending time and money on something if it won't yield results? Don't make big bets on what you *think* the customer will do, make big bets on what you *know* the customer will do. Tests move you from theory to reality.*

---

* I tested the design of this book's dust jacket—*a lot*. Go to gogetdifferent.com and get the free resources to see the video explaining my tests, the surprising findings, and the results.

I know what I am about to say is a "duh! I know that" type of thing, but knowing and doing are two different thangs. Many know this but few do it: you must plan for and measure the return on investment. For your Get Different marketing to make sense, it needs to result in a positive return. It should directly or indirectly move the thing you want to sell. And you need to ensure that your cumulative investment in time and money in marketing yields more than you spend. Marketing should pay for more than itself; it should also contribute to the ongoing health of your company. You know, your profit.

Maybe your Get Different marketing will build a prospect list with email, phone, or other contact info, without directing them to buy just yet. Maybe you offer an industry report in exchange for them providing you with their name and email. In this case you are directing them to give you contact information. Then the next stage may be selling your offer. You still need to run an ROI analysis. Other times it will be a direct offer, when they buy your product in that moment. In this case you need to calculate the ROI, too.

In the MEASURE section, note the following:

First, your INTENTIONS

START DATE—When do you plan to start your experiment?

INTENDED # OF PROSPECTS—How many prospects will you target with this experiment?

INTENDED RETURN—What is your expected ROI? It may not be actual revenue, but it may be a result (like number of sign-ups) that will support revenue.

INTENDED INVESTMENT—What is the cost to run your experiment?

Next, start your experiment by entering the OUTCOMES:

END DATE—When will your experiment end? I suggest you determine this from the start, with the understanding that things may change. You may get more or less prospect flow than expected. You may need to collect more or less data. So you may be served by extending or condensing the END DATE. Give yourself some flexibility, but not so much that the experiment fizzles.

ACTUAL # OF PROSPECTS—How many prospects actually participated in your marketing?

ACTUAL RETURN—What was your actual ROI? Like the INTENDED RETURN, it doesn't have to be revenue if that was not the intention.

ACTUAL INVESTMENT—Fill this out after you complete your experiment. What was the actual cost to run it?

With those two columns complete, review the experiment.

OBSERVATIONS—Add any notes that will help you tweak and improve your experiment, if you decide to try again or roll it out.

And as the final step, render a decision on how to proceed:

VERDICT

Now that you've completed your experiment, what's your verdict? Here are four options I consider:

Expand & Track—When your outcomes meet your intentions, have confidence that continuing the process will yield desirable results. Expand the number of prospects and increase your investment. Remember to measure along the way. Just because a Get Different Experiment works now does not mean it will work next year. Never set it and forget it. When it *is* working, milk it for all it's worth.

Retest—When you don't have confidence in the accuracy or consistency of your results, run the test again with a new sample of prospects.

Improve—When you know parts of your Get Different Experiment are working, but not all of them. This is the most common result. Aspects of your marketing may need to be improved and tested. This is when you tweak the idea to enhance the effectiveness of the DAD.

Abandon—When you know your idea is a train wreck it's time to drop it. It won't be hard for you to figure this out. If you don't yield any return or the spend can't be justified for the return. Keep a record of your experiment, but don't try to build on it or make it better. This one goes to the experiment junkyard, though you may be able to yank a part from it later when you need it for a new idea.

If it was a success, circle Expand & Track and keep it moving. If it worked but you didn't get enough data, circle Retest and run it on a new sample. If some aspects of your experiment worked but it failed to deliver, circle Improve and then fix the applicable elements of your Get Different Experiment and retry. Finally, if it bombed, circle Abandon and move on to your next experiment.

STEP 4: MEASUREMENT	INTENTIONS	OUTCOMES
	START DATE: _____	END DATE: _____
	INTENDED # OF PROSPECTS:_____	ACTUAL # OF PROSPECTS:_____
	INTENDED RETURN: _____	ACTUAL RETURN: _____
	INTENDED INVESTMENT: _____	ACTUAL INVESTMENT: _____
	OBSERVATIONS:	

VERDICT {	EXPAND & TRACK Use as ongoing strategy	RE-TEST Test new sample	IMPROVE Fix and retry	ABANDON Start new experiment

STEP 4: MEASUREMENT—The fourth and final stage of a Get Different Experiment, where the marketing intentions are set and compared with actual outcomes and a determination on how to proceed is made.

If you do bomb, don't sweat it. You're already light-years ahead of most of your competitors, if not all of them. According to an industry report by IBISWorld, there are more than fifty thousand computer service companies in operation today in the US. And none of them, since the sale of Geek Squad on October 24, 2002, have successfully marketed in any similar fashion. And the reason is blaringly obvious. They don't try. Your competition won't either. They are stuck with the "best practices" of the industry. Or the trend of the day. They are playing it as safe as they can, by blending in as much as they can. But they surely aren't trying to create different marketing that is true and authentic to them. And they surely aren't on the constant hunt to improve what they have. But you are. That's why you rock. Boom!

How Do You Know When to Stop?

Remember Gabe's story? We came up with an idea to mail a bunch of books to prospects with sticky notes pointing to helpful pages. I shared this idea with my community of Fix This Next advisers and encouraged them to try it, and add a message on the last note that read "Send me a quick text and I'll help you with any questions you have."

Not long after, I received a call from one of them. I'll call him Ted. "I followed your idea," he told me. "I sent out forty books. I got a lot of thank-yous, but no one hired me. So I guess it doesn't work."

In this case, the problem wasn't the idea. Ted stopped the campaign before he achieved statistical significance. In Chapter 3 you learned about and, I hope, came up with your Target One Hundred prospects. Ted was sixty shy of one hundred.

He also hadn't given the experiment enough time. Ted expected a response within a week, but his prospects needed at least a few weeks to go through a book and read the sticky notes. A month after he first called me, Ted called me back to say he now had two new clients. Now he's started up the campaign again.

You'll never know if your Get Different Experiment works if you give up on it before you hit statistical significance. And you need to give it enough time to do its magic. Don't start and stop. Don't rush the experiment. You'll know it's time to abandon the idea when, after trying it out for a reasonable amount of time on your Target One Hundred and tweaking the Attract and Direct components, you still aren't getting the results you had hoped to achieve.

〜〜〜

The radio spot sounded nothing like the one we scripted. It sounded "radio-y." What the hell?

If you read *Fix This Next,* you might remember Anthony Sicari, owner of New York State Solar Farm, and the story about how he uniquely leverages debt to manage cash flow.* When I met up with him at our Edison Collective mastermind,† he

---

* As an update to that story, Anthony has leveraged debt so smartly that he has eradicated all of his company's debt. He rarely borrows funds now, and only when he can spin a loan into a big win. Most of the time, he just borrows from his own cash reserve when he makes a big buy.

† If you are interested in joining our mastermind, go to mikemichalowicz.com/masterminds.

mentioned he wanted to change up his radio ads, do something different. Anthony spent roughly seventy thousand each year on that specific marketing medium for five years. After implementing *Profit First*, he couldn't justify the expense. He wanted to try radio again, because it *could* work and *could* bring in a solid ROI, but for reasons he didn't understand, it wasn't working the way he did it. Sounds like a good setup for an experiment, don't you think?

When I interviewed Anthony for this book, he told me, "I did the radio ads because I thought radio is just what business owners do, but at the end of the day, we couldn't track it. We couldn't *see* if it was working."

Together, we came up with a different concept and a plan of action.

1. **Differentiate:** Skip the canned promos with cheesy music that no one listens to and record a spot that sounds like Anthony leaving a voice mail on someone's machine. In that ad, he would explain what really pisses him off about misinformation in the solar industry, and that he is committed to fixing it.

2. **Attract:** The recording would not be some old-school weatherman reading a script with a "better put on your galoshes today" voice. It would be Anthony himself, being natural and being real. The bet was radio listeners would be more attracted to sincerity over hype.

3. **Direct:** Rather than send people to his existing website, Anthony would set up a one-page website just for this ad and Direct listeners to visit it.* That ad-specific website was the key to tracking the effectiveness of the ad.

Anthony seemed excited to get started, but after a couple of weeks, I still hadn't heard an update from him. So I messaged him and told him I'd love to hear how his radio ad turned out, and asked if he would send it to me. He did. I sighed.

It was the same old promo with the same old cheesy music. No way he could win the blink marketing moment with that ad. I have to admit, I was temporarily defeated. I can get clients and colleagues and audiences fired up to try something different with their marketing, but most of them don't follow through. It honestly hurts my heart, because I am certain it would make all the difference for them. I want to *will* them to take "risks."

Anthony could do it. I was sure of it. I just had to give it another try, to get *him* to give it another try.

"Duuuuuuude, that's not what we came up with," I told him. "You need something that shows that it's you, Anthony, the friend and neighbor who is just trying to help."

Anthony sighed. "I know. I was super pumped after I left the ideation session. I thought, 'I definitely want to implement this.' I wrote the script based on what we talked about, but when I

---

* You can see Anthony's full plan, radio scripts, and screenshots of his website at gogetdifferent.com.

tried to record it, I couldn't do it. It didn't sound natural. So, after many tries, I gave up. It just wasn't happening."

"Listen, we're going to make another one," I told him. "Are you cool with doing it the way we originally talked about?"

He was back on board.

With some minor tweaks to the script to make it sound more like the way he would actually talk in real life, Anthony shut himself in a closet, put his cell phone to one ear and a microphone to his mouth and recorded leaving the voice mail—about a hundred times. The tone was so different from every other ad he'd recorded, so outside of his comfort zone, he struggled to get it right.

Isn't it fascinating that it took Anthony more than one hundred takes to sound less like an ad and more like himself? Highlight that one, so you don't forget the effort required to deprogram that cheesy, galoshes-wearing weather caster hidden inside you. This is what happens to business owners over time. We learn how to sound and look and behave like other business owners, and then it's hard to just be ourselves.

When Anthony submitted the ad to the radio station, they urged him to make some changes. "They called me up and said, 'Can we please fix this for you for free?' They wanted it to sound more like a normal ad. I was like, no. This is what we're doing. We're running a test here. It's cool."

The radio station also tried to get Anthony to change the website he set up for the test. They wondered why he planned to drive traffic to a site that only had a video and a cell number, and no lead gen form. His marketing idea was so outside their norm, they offered to "fix it" for free. That's how uncomfortable they were with different.

Even after Anthony told them not to change his ad, they still added a voice mail ring sound and made some other changes to make it sound more "polished"—the exact opposite of the different marketing idea we'd come up with. Anthony declined this new and improved version.

"They were like, 'So, you don't want any background music, and you don't want us to chop it up, and you don't want sound effects, I told them, 'Just don't touch it.'"

The ad went live on a Monday, but the full rollout wasn't planned until Friday, so it played only a few times. Still, Anthony received a response right away. Within one day, he had two new leads. Then more started coming in. That's when he texted me, "It's working!"—with an appropriate GIF.

"I was shocked," Anthony said.

Me, not so much. I know Get Different works. You just have to experiment.

When I asked Anthony how this might change his marketing in the future, he said, "I've always felt confident on the marketing side of business, but I've never put this much effort into thinking it through before. To ask, 'Is this different?' and, 'Will this attract my ideal customer?' and, 'How can I get people to take this one specific action?' And I've learned that marketing has to be different, but it also has to be *me*. I don't want to fake anything. I want it to reflect my personality."

Now Anthony is looking at every aspect of his marketing, from social media to community engagement. He's asking those key questions, the essence of the DAD Marketing Framework.

If you haven't figured this out already, the biggest challenge you'll have isn't coming up with ideas; it's executing ideas. Marketing guru and author Seth Godin calls this state of mind "the dip," which happens after you come up with an idea and get excited to try it. You feel a dip in enthusiasm and start to doubt yourself. It is my intention that the Get Different Experiments will help you navigate yourself out of the dip pretty quickly because they are not big marketing initiatives that need months of planning before execution. When you experiment, you try fast, and you also fail or find something with potential fast. Experiment fast but don't rush the results. Like Ted's experiment, the nature of the marketing takes the prospect longer to comply with the Direct. Start your next Get Different Experiment now! And, if you find you still need a nudge, here are some tips to help you move forward:

- Do your experiment along with others. Because we fear rejection from our industry, creating a new group of "Different Doers" will combat that *and* serve as accountability. Kasey Compton of Mindsight PLLC, has a group of eight mental health professionals who support each other in trying new things. Most of them want to increase their lead flow. They've executed some different marketing ideas. Cymbria launched a "COVID SUCKS" campaign. Heather started doing mental health sessions with her dog on TikTok. Kasey tried reverse graffiti. And you already know one success story from that group: Ernestina Perez's *90 Day Fiancé* video experiment, which I shared in Chapter 4.

- Take action fast. The more time you give yourself to think about your idea, the less likely you are to do it. I'd rather you have a failed, half-assed experiment, than a potentially successful one that never happens. I am not telling you to cut corners in your Get Different Experiment, because that will greatly increase the risk of failure and undermine your confidence. I am simply saying that a half-baked idea is still an idea, and if you are waiting for the perfect idea to present itself, we are now experiencing the biggest cost of all: lost time. Doing beats perfection every time.

- Start with the smallest, easiest element of your different idea and build from there. Remember Justin Wise's advice about breaking down each step so you can do step one today.

- Turn fear on itself. Rather than get caught up in the negative what-ifs, worrying about what could happen if you try this, ask yourself, "What is the cost of *not* doing this?"

- And, if you want to make sure you are doing Get Different right, you can check out our services at differentcompany.co.

When speaking to a group of young entrepreneurs at Y Combinator's Startup School in Palo Alto, Mark Zuckerberg, a founder of Facebook, said, "In a world that's changing really quickly, the only strategy that is guaranteed to fail is not taking risks." Marketing is about failing quickly and small-ly enough that you rapidly find what works. Expect ten fails for every one success in supertargeted marketing. Expect one hundred or one thousand fails for every one success in more high-volume, low-cost marketing. Shoot, a billboard may have five hundred thousand misses for only one hit and still be well worth it. You just won't know what that success will be until you try them out. So get busy and do; don't perfect. You'll find out pretty quickly whether your winning different approach worked, because you will follow through, my friend. I believe in you.

Your Turn

Do the thing. And for the sake of all that is holy, don't wait until conditions are perfect. There's no such thing as perfect. Before the day is out, plan your first Get Different Experiment, do the first step on your list, and keep it moving. If you have a team, or an assistant, pass the list on to them and have *them* implement it. And if you are saying it's too late in the day, you're bullshitting me (and yourself), because you are reading this right now. Do that next step, now!

If you are still stuck, or are just continuing to read without doing the work, I will give you four ideas right now. You must do one. Any one of these takes less than five minutes to do. All are likely different from what you typically do. All will build your Different Doer muscle. Are you ready?

1. Find a blank, full-size piece of printer paper. With a marker, write a letter to a Target One Hundred prospect that reads "I realize you don't know me, but I was thinking of you today. I am just so impressed by what you have achieved with your business. Wishing you continued success." At the end of your note put your name and cell number. Also note that your line complimenting them must be truly about them. If they don't own a business, don't write "what you have achieved with your business." Include something relevant to them and authentic to you.

2. Make a video of you saying the same stuff as in option one. You can use your smartphone or some online program. Email the video to your prospect, with a subject line that reads "I made you a personal video (I swear)."

3. With the Target One Hundred prospect identified, find something they personally like or are affiliated with. An online bio or social media page often has all you need. Then get them a gift that is linked to their likes and mail it to them with a note that says, "I saw that you are a fan of [their field of interest]. I know this is out of the blue, but I couldn't pass up on sending this to you. Enjoy!" At the end of the note put your name and cell number. If you were prospecting me, you could discover quickly that I like Virginia Tech football, hair bands from the eighties, and hiking with my dog. So a note with "I saw that you are a fan of hiking with your

dog" and the gift being a Virginia Tech (or Def Leppard) dog collar would get my attention.

4. Pick up the phone and call. Simply say this into voice mail: "Hi, I'm [your name]. I admire your business and what you do. Honestly, you would be a dream client for me. I want to reach out to you and let you know that, if you are willing to connect, I will do everything to provide you with a level of [experience/service/product] you have never had before. My company is [your company name]. My cell is [cell number]. Please call or text me back so we can chat. Thanks so much." If you are so terrified by this different marketing, just note that 99.9 percent of the time you will get voice mail. The other 0.1 percent of the time you hit gold.

There you have it. You can do your own Get Different Experiment now. Or you can pick from one of the four ideas I shared above. No matter what, you must do one now.

Make sure you download the Get Different Experiment Sheet at gogetdifferent.com. Rebels can use a blank piece of paper. Follow the steps outlined above. Rinse. Repeat.

My Turn

I'm not sure if you are as giddy as I am for this moment. It's rubber-to-the-road time. And I did it with my tree bookcase. Here is what I documented. Can you guess my verdict?

INTENTIONS	OUTCOMES
START DATE: _____	END DATE: _____
INTENDED # OF PROSPECTS:_____	ACTUAL # OF PROSPECTS:_____
INTENDED RETURN: _____	ACTUAL RETURN: _____
INTENDED INVESTMENT: _____	ACTUAL INVESTMENT: _____

OBSERVATIONS:

VERDICT {

EXPAND & TRACK	RE-TEST	IMPROVE	ABANDON
Use as ongoing strategy	Test new sample	Fix and retry	Start new experiment

STEP 4: MEASUREMENT

STEP 4: MEASUREMENT—The fourth and final stage of a Get Different Experiment, where the marketing intentions are set and compared with actual outcomes and a determination on how to proceed is made.

INTENTIONS

Start Date: March 29, 2020

Intended # of Prospects: 2,000 (250 per week)

Intended Return: 400 new book sales

Intended Investment: Onetime $1,750 for the shelf/book holders

Note on Back of Sheet: I originally estimated $1,200 for the bookcase. The best size for the space would cost $1,725. The holders were around $25.

OUTCOMES

End Date: May 24, 2020

Actual # of Prospects: 4,000 (500 per week)

Actual Return: 516 books documented (more?)

Actual Investment: Onetime $2,200 (needed lights too)

Observations:

The actual presentations via video skyrocketed because of the COVID pandemic. The conversion was lower than expected, but as I refined the ask it increased. Changed the ask to be buy the book _and_ you are supporting me. Capture video chats to see what people are saying. Mention

the tree during presentation to reiterate what
they already see.

Verdict: IMPROVE Fix and Retry. The tweak is
simply the ask needs to have a personal
justification, not just that it will benefit the
prospect.

Did you guess the verdict? It is rare that you get it right
the first time. This experiment in fact went much better than
most for me; I had more initial success than usual. Woo-hoo!
And with minor tweaks I was able to get 23 percent of an at-
tending live audience to buy my books in the moment—with
permission from the host—because of the tree. It is now a standard marketing practice for me, until others duplicate and dilute. But that is okay, I already have other tests I am running,
and think I have something that will move a whole lot more
books.

CHAPTER EIGHT

How to Know It's Working

T rust wallets, not words."

As I grew Olmec Systems, I had a ton of "great ideas"—that no one wanted. People would tell me they liked my new offer. My closest friends would say they loved my new approach. As I asked folks about a new product in development, they would say, "I'd buy that in a heartbeat." But when it came time to pony up, those same people wouldn't follow through. People just weren't buying, and my frustration was through the roof. I had a great idea. They said they wanted it, after all! What the hell did I do wrong?

I asked Frank Minutolo, my business mentor, what I should do. That's when he shared those four words of wisdom, which I have carried with me ever since. Trust wallets, not words. I still seek direction and feedback; I still listen to people. Now, though,

I know I'm far too biased about my own brainstorms. And get this—so are most people.

When someone tells you what they think you want to hear, they aren't doing it to mess with you; they think they are performing a service by encouraging you. But don't kid yourself. "I would buy that in a heartbeat" does not mean that person will actually buy your product. What it actually means is "I want you to like me." More than that, though, people want to avoid conflict. They don't want to argue with you or hurt your feelings. So, prospects, friends, customers, even colleagues will end up telling you something is a "good idea" when it's really, really not. And they say, "I'd buy that"—even when they absolutely wouldn't.

So I run tests on my ideas to judge interest by *actual* interest, demand by *actual* demand, to determine whether people would be willing to pay for something by *actually* paying for something. When it's clear a new product idea isn't viable, or a new marketing approach isn't working, I cut bait and save myself a heap of heartache and wasted resources.

Do I always remember to follow Frank's advice? Of course not. Sometimes, my unbridled enthusiasm for my "brilliant" idea overrides reason and, forgetting to trust in wallets, instead I swallow the words hook, line, and stinker. As far as love languages* go, I'm a "words of affirmation" guy through and through, so if someone has a favorable comment about one of my crazy notions, I have a strong tendency to be all over it. I develop, do, and

---

* If you are not familiar with the book *The 5 Love Languages* by Gary Chapman, I encourage you to read it stat. It will help you with all forms of communication, including with loved ones, colleagues, and prospects!

spend, knowing this next thing will be the hot thing. But the reality is I *don't* know. Words are cheap. Only when I can get people to part with their cash do I really know if I have something desirable.

You hear what you want to hear, and you believe it, because your peeps told you so. When you trust words over wallets, you expend resources on an idea, product, or service that very few people—if anyone—will actually want. To prevent this, measure actual actions.

In this chapter, you'll learn how to track your marketing experiment to see whether you can roll it out right away, it needs improving, or you should ditch it entirely because it was an epic fail.

Do Strangers Love Your Thing?

I feel the need to qualify the "wallets over words" strategy: Friends buying your stuff doesn't count. They want to support you. They want to see you succeed. More than that, they really want to stay your friend, and this means they're not going to do anything to hurt your feelings. So they open up their pandering wallets as they say what you want to hear and make the investment necessary to maintain harmony and friendship, not because they want the shit you're selling.

My friend Jayden is known for his homemade meatballs the size of hamburgers. He brings them to every potluck, serves them at every party he hosts. One day, he told a group of us, "Hey, I'm thinking about selling Jayden's Big Boy meatballs. Everyone loves them when I cook them at home, so I'm going to make them for supermarkets."

Of course, everyone said, "That's a great idea! "And the deceptive, dangerous "if I owned a supermarket, I would totally buy your meatballs" accolades flowed. Believing that chorus of approval, backed by the ring of "if I was . . ." hypotheticals, was Jayden's first mistake.

Bolstered by their confirmation, he rented a commercial kitchen, bought supplies and ingredients. Five thousand dollars later, he had two hundred meatballs that didn't taste quite right. Turns out cooking a few meatballs at home doesn't scale to cooking large volumes in a commercial kitchen. So Jayden changed the recipe. He invested money in improving the process, and when he was finally satisfied he'd made a good, supermarket-ready meatball, he came back to our group for a taste test. When he asked how we liked them, everyone chimed in with positive comments. "Like home," and "loved them!" and "good for you, Jayden!"

Then Jayden asked his friends if they would buy the meatballs. Again, he received only positive feedback. "Of course!" and "heck yes!" and "no question!"

As the quantities changed, the recipe continued to change. Jayden spent another five grand on more tests and on packaging prototypes. Then he brought it back to our group. This time, he asked us to buy the meatballs. Everyone dropped sixty bucks on a couple of packages. Jayden was thrilled. He'd made more money in sales in thirty minutes than he earned in one day at his job. He was all in.

His friends loved his meatballs. His friends all bought his meatballs.

It was obvious his meatball business would be a great success.

Deep-voiced, movie narrator guy: "He was wrong. Dead wrong."

You're a savvy business owner; you can see what's coming, right?

Jayden quit his job and found a month-to-month lease on a commercial kitchen. He invested in the gear he needed: big pots, even bigger mixers. He leased two massive refrigerators and installed a row of stoves. He slogged through the inspections, tweaked the vacuum-seal packaging, and worked night and day to get his meatballs to market.

Two months and seventy-five thousand dollars later, he was ready to launch. The first batch of meatballs came off the line—twenty-four hundred oversize meatballs, packed in boxes of twelve. He ventured out to supermarkets and restaurants looking for buyers, but—movie narrator voice again—no one wanted them. He had meeting after meeting, but even after people sampled the meatballs, they always declined.

Desperate, he came back to us, his friends, and said, "I made extra packages. Who wants to buy?" This time, he heard a different set of comments. "I still have some left" and "sorry, man, but I am meatballed out at the moment" and "I want to wait until the holidays."

Undeterred, Jayden pushed harder. He went after more stores, more restaurants. Still, no one wanted his meatballs. He did get our local supermarket to take a few packages on consignment, but they sold only three units in four weeks.

Ninety days after he had first asked his friends if they liked his meatball business idea, his life savings gone, Jayden had to accept that he was done. His dream of being a business owner had failed, because he bet on the feedback from his friends. His "proof" wasn't proof at all.

Incidentally, I was one of the few dissenters. I mean, who buys a twelve pack of hamburger-size meatballs? When I cook for my family of five, we might need eight meatballs if we plan to have leftovers. But twelve? Who on this planet wants to drop thirty-something bucks on a huge pack of meatballs, no matter how good they taste?

Jayden didn't pass the Direct stage (the second *D* in DAD). He asked for too much, too soon. Sell two Big Boy meatballs, maybe three, but twelve? No. In fact, I did a quick web search to ask, "What is the cost for a twelve-pack of meatballs?" And the Google search came back with "What the fuck? Who buys that?" Then the entire internet crashed.

Please don't bank on nice comments from the people who love you. When they buy from you, consider it a donation, not proof that they genuinely love your thing. When people you know say your marketing is great, they can't see past their own bias of loving you, or not wanting to offend you, or both. The truth comes from strangers, always. If you get people who don't know you and don't care about how you feel taking the action you want, then and only then do you know you have something. Get strangers buying. That's proof.

Confirm your marketing idea works by asking your target prospects (i.e., strangers) for money up front. Get a deposit, or even the full amount. If people aren't willing to put money down, you know from their actions that they don't see value in your offer. Sure, it's always a good idea to get feedback about your ideas from people you trust, but only if they are willing to share hard truths over comfortable lies. Because if the people you trust are sharing comfortable lies, then guess what? You can't trust them.

Even if your marketing is about moving people through steps to the ultimate sale, you can test people by having a "currency" exchange. If you are giving a free PDF, don't send it out willy-nilly. Ask strangers to give you something in exchange—an email, a phone number, a buck. You get the truth through currency exchanges with strangers. When asking friends, there is a whole other level of consideration and confusion: the bond of your friendship, social grace, and too often being told what you want to hear over what you need to hear.

Test Now

On Monday, January 13, Austin Karp offered up a marketing idea.

On Tuesday, January 14, Austin's idea was up and running.

His first day as an intern for the Savannah Bananas, Austin raised his hand in their weekly brainstorm meeting and said, "What if when we call customers to thank them for buying a ticket, we thank them with a rap?"

Ever since they started their franchise, the Savannah Bananas have been calling customers to thank them for their ticket purchase. Yes, they call every single person. That's Get Different applied to customer service.

Jesse, who still makes many of the calls himself, said, "Interesting idea. Proceed."

He didn't say, "let's discuss it."

He didn't say, "yeah, but . . ."

He didn't say, "okay, who wants to do it?" followed by stone-cold silence.

Jesse did a quick DAD test in his head.

A phone call or voice mail, rapped? Differentiate test, passed.

Would people think this is the newest Nigerian prince scam? Probably not.

Getting a message saying, "This is the Savannah Bananas, thanks for getting tickets. We have a little rap for you . . ." was engaging, funny, and just weird enough to keep curiosity flowing. Attract test, likely a pass.

The goal was to get people excited to go to a game. It was unlikely that a thank-you rap song would cause people to regret their purchase; instead it would likely get people excited for the fun they would experience at the ballpark. Likely action of the customer: attend the game. Direct test, passed.

Jesse knows the secret to Get Different marketing is to ask, "Does DAD approve?" every time, and to do it quickly so you can find out whether it's worth your time or not. Don't get bogged down. Get testing fast. The data will point to the effectiveness. DAD is new to you, so it may initially take a few minutes to sort through it and get to the go or no-go decision. Jesse has it down to seconds, and with practice you will, too. So, the decision to proceed with a "rap thank-you" test happened within ten seconds of the idea being raised.

"But . . . I don't sing," Austin replied. "And I'm really awkward at rapping. Like, *really* awkward."

Jesse grinned. "Even better. You are now Austin the Awkward Rapper."

At the Savannah Bananas brainstorm meetings, the goal is to execute ideas within twenty-four hours. Twenty-four hours, my friend. That's from concept to active implementation, within one night's sleep (or five Red Bulls). Jesse knows that action trumps contemplation and the proof is in the pudding—ticket and merch sales. He wants ideas up and running the very next day so he can find out from *actual customers* if the idea works. So he collects the data, and if the test works, then he goes big with it. If it flops, no big deal. Then he knows he found something that doesn't work, and he's onto other ideas, other tests.

"The problem with traditional ideation and creative brainstorming," Jesse explained, "is that it dies there. No one is assigned to lead it. No one takes action. It just goes in the closet with the countless other long-forgotten 'great' ideas. An idea is only great once it is executed upon."

According to Jesse, the Savannah Bananas have a rule: "The person who creates the idea owns it. Unless someone else makes an argument as to why they should have it, the idea stays with the creator for its initial launch." But though they may lead the effort on their project, it's not only up to them; their entire team needs to do different. Jesse's goal is for *everyone* to pitch in and build their Get Different muscle.

Austin made his first thank-you rap call the morning after he came up with the idea. Some listened and laughed, others played their rap voice mail to friends, and one fan even sent a rap back. Point being, it got engagement. Nothing huge. But what self-respecting Savannah Bananas fan, the great lovers of all things silly, wouldn't want to listen to an awkward intern rapping—awkwardly?

Jesse told me that they now have the entire ticketing staff doing rap thank-yous this upcoming season. Austin's different marketing made it past the Get Different Experiment Sheet, now stamped Expand & Track. In other words, the awkward rap is now part of the Bananas' marketing plan. Because they have always personally called everyone who buys a ticket, the estimated cost is less than ten seconds of additional time on each phone call. The return, while extremely hard to measure in sales or concession stand purchases, is based on the many social media posts about the rap. It has inspired more fans to talk to their friends about the Bananas. And aside from the COVID-19 situation, the Bananas sell out every season.

You've probably heard the saying "He who hesitates is lost." Let's modernize it—*we* who hesitate are lost. Because we are. Lost in a vast sea of sameness. Lost in the purgatory where good ideas and good intentions go to die. Lost in entrepreneurial poverty. So don't hesitate to take action and launch your next Get Different Experiment. Challenge yourself—or your team—to get moving on it within twenty-four hours. Or, if you need a little more time to gather resources, or make something, or whatever, take one week. But no longer than that. Test now. Test fast.

I researched for this book over ten years, and the feedback is clear. Jeff Walker, Jesse Cole, Ernestina Perez, Anthony Sicari, Kasey Anton, Gabriel Piña, and every person who proves to be a marketing genius consistently does one thing: they test their idea fast so they can get confirmation that it worked, fast. They know the risk is in the *not* doing, in hypothesizing and relying on advice and opinions over actual results. So they don't screw around. They set up a test and they get it done. You must, too.

The OMEN Method for Marketing

This method for tracking Get Different Experiment success sounds dark—okay, it sounds *ominous*—but it's really just an acronym. I first introduced the OMEN Method in my book *Fix This Next*, which helps you determine which vital change will truly level up your business.

OMEN breaks down like this:

> **Objective.** What is the intended outcome? For example, do you want more qualified customers? Do you want new subscribers for your mailing list or social media channel? Do you want people to promote your offer for you? Remember the Win of your marketing is the ultimate outcome you seek. Sometimes, though, the Win will take a few steps, and you want to Direct your prospects to take one specific action, not a sequence of actions. The Objective of your experiment is the first step that moves you to the Win.

> **Measurements.** What defines a successful outcome? For example, do you need ten new customers per week who will spend at least five hundred dollars per transaction?

Do you want fifty new subscribers? Do you want one thousand people to promote your thing?

Evaluation Frequency. How often will you measure the progress? Most business owners are great at setting the Objective and Measurements around it, but then "set it and forget it." They identify a goal and then go on with their day-to-day, only realizing months later that they are off track. "Oh yeah, what ever happened to that project?" This is like saying your goal is to lose ten pounds this year, and then the New Year rolls around and you discover you've actually *gained* five. Make your progress check-ins a calendared event. Schedule them to track it.

Nurture. How will you reevaluate your settings? When you check in on your progress, what could you tweak to improve your outcomes? Were the Objective and Measurements you set the right ones? As time has moved forward and you are evaluating your progress, are you seeing elements that need to be changed, tweaked, amplified, or abandoned? Make those changes and continue.

Robin Robins is one of the most impressive marketers I have ever known. Even her name is a stroke of marketing genius. It's easy to remember and curiosity invoking. Well played, Robin. Well played.

For Robin, the change to her marketing was as simple as adding one of those business nameplates you see on people's desks to a virtual desk. She created a marketing program that she calls

Shock & Awe. In developing the process, she set up an experiment with a customized web page for each target prospect. First, they would get a piece of snail mail inviting them to visit a web page created just for them. When they went to the site, it had a virtual desk complete with a phone, tablet, business cards—all the standard stuff you would see on someone's actual office desk.

The results were meh. People went to the page, but it didn't convert to the prospect inquiries she had targeted. But Robin is known as The Relentless Redhead because of her red hair and that she never gives up. She had the web designer add a nameplate with the prospect's name to the screen in big, bold letters, right up top. It was the ultimate in personalization. That is how you nurture your Get Different marketing. And that is how Robin improved web page conversions by more than 200 percent.

Remember, just because you roll out your Get Different Experiment does not mean it is perfected. Listen to people's actions, compare them to your Objective and Measurements, and nurture accordingly.

In *Fix This Next*, I explain that just as humans have a hierarchy of needs, so do businesses. Before we can think about feeling fulfilled, we first need to make sure we can actually breathe. That we aren't starving. That we're safe. For business, that first base level is sales. Without revenue, we've got nothin'. And sales starts with marketing. In other words, marketing matters. A lot. Please, and this is a big-ass please, set your metrics to focus on marketing that drives sales.

Persuasion strategist, and one of the most authentic and different marketers I know, Bushra Azhar said, "Your business runs on sales. Not likes. Not fans. Not followers. Not email addresses. None of that—only sales. So, market every day. Market with pride. Market with integrity. Market with enthusiasm. Get better at it. Make tons of offers. Follow up. Nudge people. Remind them what they stand to miss, and do it as if your business depends on it. Because it does."

Your business depends on sales. And your sales depend on marketing, so let's make sure your Get Different Experiment serves that vital need.

Key Your Marketing

Direct marketers use a technique that all of us should use: the key. For each marketing campaign, they insert a unique and trackable action, rather than the same action for all campaigns. So, for example, let's say you want people to buy your product that helps them stop vaping. To do that, you send out two different mailers. The first mailer is a picture of a baby smoking a cigar with a message that reads "Vaping is even worse. Go to stopvapingfast.com." The second mailer is a picture of an elderly, wrinkled woman vaping, with a picture that reads "Sarah is twenty-two years old! Go to neverevervape.com."

Notice that each ad directs people to go to a website for more information, but the ads have different keys—the different URLs. One ad goes to stopvapingfast.com and the other goes to neverevervape.com. By tracking the click-throughs to each site, you can figure out which ad works best. That is the use of a key, where each marketing campaign can be distinctly measured because it ties to a specific Direct, even—scratch that, *especially*—when the prospect is not aware of the key.

Remember the radio ad by my friend Anthony Sicari? He set up a key for that radio ad by sending people to solaranthony.com. Because it's the only ad that sends people there, he can measure the results of that ad. Simple!

You need to know what works and what doesn't work, so add a key whenever possible to your marketing so you can easily track the results that your marketing drives. You can key with distinct websites and phone numbers, phone numbers with different extensions, mailing addresses with different "suite" numbers, unique coupon codes—and so much more.

Even if your directive is to ask people to show up somewhere in person, you can change the meeting place based on the ad to see which one worked. For example, let's say you wanted to get a bunch of people to show up to the local park for an event. You have three different marketing experiments you want to try, and for each one, you key a different meetup location in the park—the entrance, the gazebo, the pond. Then you keep track of how many people show up to each location. Now you know which ad worked best to get people out to your event.

In case you have never used a key before, know they have been used on you. Have you ever heard a radio commercial or podcast where the ad ends with "tell them Joe sent you to get 10 percent off"? Joe is a key. Anthony Sicari's ad-specific website is the key.

Ever see the same ad pop up all over every website you visited? In that case, the key is called a cookie. It was put on your computer when you looked at that new car or whatever. Now advertisers know what website initiated your interest, and they use that cookie to keep putting ads in front of you. A key is used to know which marketing triggered your prospect's interest so that you can use the data to better market to other prospects and improve your odds of converting. The more you know about your prospect, the easier it is to sell to them. And the more you know where they came from, the easier it is to learn more about your prospect and leverage that to your marketing advantage. The key is the key.

∿∿∿

Jason Iverson's first Get Different Experiment failed. The owner of Iverson's Barber Shop in Sacramento, he, like so many in the grooming industry, faced a huge drop in business during the COVID-19 lockdowns. Even after restrictions were lifted and he was allowed to reopen, business was down 30 percent. People now worked from home, and so stopping by the barbershop on the way home from work was not commonplace. Other people had learned how to cut their own hair so they could stay home, or had a family member do it for them. Barely able to cover basic expenses, Jason needed twenty to thirty new clients each week to get back on track.

He tried a Get Different Experiment based on reaching a target demographic no one seemed to be catering to—the people who run the Spartan Race. Have you seen them? They are hardcore, the envy of every speedwalker. Jason noticed that the Spartans would come into his barbershop to get a Mohawk cut the

Friday before the Saturday race, and then come *back* into the shop on Sunday to trim it up for work on Monday. So Jason partnered with gym owners and gave it a shot—a discount here (Jason's shop) and a discount there (gym's). No one responded. He tried labeling a special "off-menu" cut called the "Spartan Spike" and invited his gym owner partners to share this as an exclusive offer, affording the gym members a sense of priority and importance and specialness that they only get by being part of the gym. Yet again, no one responded. If not for the pandemic, I would have advised him to keep tweaking the experiment, because he already had proof that people wanted the haircuts. The uncertainty about whether or not the Spartan races would actually happen was an obstacle he could not overcome.

This is where many people would give up and return to marketing mediocrity. Not Jason, though. He went back to the drawing board. He decided to try a different demographic—people who want their hair cut and who are very concerned about contracting COVID-19 and passing it on to loved ones. Jason knew all about that fear. He cared for his mother, who was a serious risk for complications should she contract the virus. As a result, he had implemented additional safety protocols at his barbershop, beyond those required by law. Jason created a video explaining these protocols and the hospital-grade cleaning and disinfecting sprays and products he used, and that the health of his clients and his team was his biggest priority. He didn't just promote clean cuts; he promoted *clean* clean cuts.

This time, it worked. Within a few days, he had three new inquiries about setting up appointments. And he noted that his existing clients actively talked with each other about the

COVID-19 precautions Iverson's Barber Shop had taken. This meant the same dialogue was likely happening among friends, too.

Fails happen. It's the natural order of marketing—and they are the key to your greatness. Because a fail means you tried. Not trying means you're dead in the water before you even begin. At the same time, minor gains are the norm. Eventually, they add up to big wins.

Jason didn't have people lined up, socially distanced six feet apart, trying to get in. His new initiative resulted in three new people in just as many days. Even though he didn't hit a home run with his new marketing idea, he got on base. This is a verdict of IMPROVE—Fix & Retry. He found something with potential, just not the panacea.

Think about lifting weights to gain muscle. You don't get all ripped overnight. You need to build it over time, through resistance. You get stronger by confronting the pain, not by avoiding it. You gain where there is pain.

I know I grow when I face criticism and the pain of failure. Still, I have to get over myself nearly every single time. It's not like I wake up, beat my chest, and shout, "I am the greatest," before heading off to take eighteen risks that day. I mean, if I did *any* of that I probably wouldn't have a single friend. No, my inner dialogue is probably pretty close to yours when it comes to taking marketing risks: (1) I have an idea, (2) I think it's better than sliced bread, (3) I figure out the time and effort I'll need to put into doing it, (4) I let the worry build by wondering what other people will think, and (5) I use this as an excuse not to do it by justifying that it will be too hard or "a waste of time," and then (6) I walk away from my idea or half-ass it and (7) use my lack of effort toward doing different to prove that different doesn't work.

To get past this negative thought process, I take inspiration from the people and companies I love. Fact: the best hair band ever is Def Leppard. I will fight you on this. *But,* about 90 percent of their songs suck. They have more than one hundred songs you've never heard, and that's a good thing even to a little-too-into-Leppard fan like me. You can't get that time back. Still, I believe they are the greatest hair band of all time, despite the fact they produced the song "Unbelievable," which is, well, unbelievably bad. Some of your marketing "songs" will be unbelievable, too—unbelievable flops. Most will never be heard by more than a few folks who happened to tune in. Some may actually suck so bad that they don't get any airtime (traction) at all. That's okay. It's the nature of creation. The key is to keep producing, keep trying, keep taking risks, because while some of your experiments will be epic fails, others will be epic successes. Massive. I'm talking "Rock of Ages"–level success. You just need to put your stuff out there, track it, and keep it rolling even if success feels "Unbelievable." Did I mention how much that song sucks?

Your Turn

Time to run three more fast experiments. Yeah, I said three:

1. Complete a Get Different Experiment Sheet for the next product you see. Literally whatever you notice

next. If you are at a desk, it could be a USB drive or a letter opener, or that weird Xikezan beard straightener that is still on my desk. If you are listening in your car, it could be your car, or cell phone, or that cold cup of coffee. If you are out spartan-racing, it could be, well, let's see—Mohawk haircuts.

2.   That first one was to simply go through the experience of completing the sheet again. This next one is for you to market yourself, again. Pick the worst performing product or service in your business. The one that just doesn't sell. Or doesn't sell well. Run a Get Different Experiment on it. Complete the sheet, do the test (for real), and render a verdict. But the verdict may only happen after you did the experiment fully. No half-assing.

3.   Conduct the third experiment on the thing that gets the most word-of-mouth business. If nothing gets word of mouth, which one do you talk about most? (That is word of your mouth.) Conduct a Get Different Experiment for this thing. If it gets the most word of mouth, it is likely to be your best offer, or at least what you are most known for among your existing clients. Marketing what you are already known for has an amplification effect. Now you have both your cake (active Get Different marketing) and icing (word of mouth).

~~~~~~~~~~~~~

CHAPTER NINE

The Disadvantage Advantage

Here's something I learned about squirrels: They are really bad at remembering their hiding places. You've probably seen them haul off with acorns. You may have even sat in a park long enough to watch them bury their food in the ground. Turns out, they're just like me trying to find my car keys. Or worse, me trying to find my *car* in a mall parking lot. I step outside and draw a complete blank. So do squirrels.

Studies show that they forget where they hide about 74 percent of the nuts they buried. (Who is the crackpot who tracks stuff like this? And what other secrets to the working of the universe do they hold?) The fact that squirrels don't have a clue where they leave *most* of their food kind of makes all of that frantic pre-winter food hoarding seem pointless, right? Not true, say the researchers. Turns out, they are the "inadvertent heroes of forest restoration."[1] Their perceived weakness is actually really good for trees. Every lost acorn can become a mighty oak. Do I think squirrels maybe need a "find your nuts" coach to help them increase their averages? Nah. They probably know they suck at finding their stash and have adjusted accordingly—hence all the hoarding. In truth, their weakness is actually a strength.

The squirrels adequately feed themselves, and they thrive as a community—and at planting trees. The trees serve the planet, the planet benefits from cleaner air, carbon dioxide reduction, and other good stuff. And those squirrels? They're creating a habitat for their future generations; they need trees to nest and forage. As much as it pains me to say, because they love to bolt in front of my car when I least expect it, causing me to grind my brakes into the floor, squirrels are the do-gooders of the woods.

I realize I've made my point with one story, but please indulge me with another one that really drives that point home. UC Davis knows the power of trees. Its campus has lots of them—olive trees, to be exact. The trees, which are famously beautiful, enhanced the walking path below until a nuisance presented itself. The problem had nothing to do with squirrels, though. It was the Slip 'n Slide on the sidewalks after the olives fell off the trees. Greasy sidewalks made for lots of accidents, and so for years, the groundskeepers hustled to pick up the olive crop each season.

In 2005, the campus grounds manager, Sal Genito, got an idea. Genito thought, "When life give me olives, why not make olive oil?" Instead of cutting down the trees and disposing of the "problem," he proposed transforming the problem into an opportunity. He and an assembled crew started harvesting the olives to make olive oil! The first harvest of olive oil sold out within a day. Now, UC Davis is known for its famous olive oil. But my favorite part? The university sells more than one hundred twenty-five gallons of olive oil every year, creating enough revenue for the harvesting and bottling to be self-funded and saving another sixty thousand a year that the campus was previously paying for cleanup and accident resolution.

Sometimes, we hold ourselves back from really going all out with our marketing because we think we have some sort of disadvantage, that we don't measure up to our competition in some way. We see the disadvantage as something that needs to be covered up or, as in UC Davis's case, cleaned up. The thing is, what we *think* is a disadvantage very often is actually an advantage. In fact, it could be the very thing that differentiates us from the competition, the inspiration for some stellar, out-of-the-box marketing.

Would you consider a twenty-five-thousand-dollar oil change a deterrent to buying the car that requires it? I would.

The Bugatti Veyron oil change takes more than twenty-four hours to complete and costs upwards of twenty-five thousand bucks, and yet the car still sells. Some online forums report you can get the oil change for twenty-one thousand, if you have a coupon or vow that you will never admit to once owning a Kia. It is this oddity of opulence that becomes magnetic marketing. You may never aspire to own a Bugatti, but the brand may now own part of your brain space because Bugatti highlights its oil change "weakness."

This lube service that could be considered "gouging," "ridiculous," or "a joke" has been repositioned for the brand's ideal prospect to view it as "prestigious," and "necessary for the finer life," and "a privilege for the elite." Instead of being a deterrent, it is a "call to arms" to the filthy rich who can afford to spend that every three thousand miles. You need to re-up for the opulent club with every oil change. For the price of just one Bugatti lube job, you could buy a brand-new Toyota Corolla. You won't find any news stories about the forty-dollar oil change you can get on your Honda. But there are a chunk of news stories—and huge buzz—about the *elite* Bugatti.

A simple reframe of your disadvantage can help you find the courage to do your own Get Different Experiments. *And* the stuff you don't want anyone to know about, the stuff that you think needs to be fixed, hidden, or downplayed, could be a starting point for you to brainstorm new different marketing ideas. So flip the narrative. You're not a forgetful squirrel. You're a forestation superhero.

The Magic of Mistakes

"For five years, I had a dirty little secret," my buddy Matt Shoup told me. "I vowed to never share this secret with anybody. Ever. This information placed in the wrong hands or perceived in the wrong way could have completely destroyed my company."

Then, one day, he revealed it.

Matt owns a house painting business, M & E Painting. He shared his story with me.

"I was on my final paint estimate of the day, ready to close the deal," Matt started. "The customer had had a bad experience with his last painter. They were late, made a mess, and did terrible work."

So Matt showed the customer his marketing brochure, and turned right to the testimonials page. "We had a near-perfect 98.6 percent customer satisfaction rating, and had served more than four thousand people in our first eight years in business."

The glossy marketing piece should have sealed the deal, except just as Matt handed his customer the pen to sign the contract, the customer interrupted him. "He was a pull-no-punches sort of guy. He said, 'Matt, that shiny marketing brochure is crap. You think for a second you'd ever put a bad referral in there? Where is the page with the pissed-off customers? You want my business, I suggest you start telling me one of those stories.'"

Now, you should know that Matt is a superconfident guy. He's not afraid to try new things, not afraid to have difficult conversations, and he's absolutely not afraid to go after the sale. He shows up prepared to answer any question you may have. Except this customer had asked him to share a bad story. A really bad story. And Matt had one—except it was a secret. A really, *really* bad secret.

So Matt told his customer something else. "I shared a weak story about a time I painted the wrong color on a house. He called BS. Then I told him how we painted the *right* color on the *wrong* house. Oops."

Matt's customer still wasn't satisfied. Sure, those mistakes were pretty bad. But not really different from the competition's mistakes. The customer pushed to hear a story of a mistake that no one else makes and how Matt and his team handled that.

Admittedly this was not your typical sales meeting, and other less confident minds may have walked away. But Matt doesn't like to lose. Ever. So, he dug deep on his biggest F-up.

That's when Matt blurted, "Well, since we're at it, let me tell you about the time I painted a baby."

Yup. Matt's team painted a baby.

Dirty secret revealed.

See, five years earlier, Matt got a phone call from one of his guys on a job site.

"Raul said, 'Mateo, Mateo, Mateo, you need to get over here real quick, man. We were painting the door, and the customer was there, and the baby was there, and things are bad. I mean, the lady, the paint, the baby, boom!'"

The first thing Matt did was ask if the baby was okay and if the customers were okay. Thankfully, no one was hurt. Then he got in his car and drove to the job site.

"We were painting trims and doors for a couple in Windsor," Matt explained. "There was a door that entered through the back of the garage, and Raul was getting ready to spray it black. He loaded his paint sprayer, stood about a foot away from the door, and pulled the trigger. The thing he didn't know was that the homeowner was standing a few feet behind him holding her nine-month-old baby girl. The other thing he didn't know was that the spray gun's tip was jammed. So as soon he pulled the trigger, boom! It exploded and splattered paint everywhere!"

Everything was covered in black paint: the walls of the house, the concrete floor, the patio furniture, the deck, the fence, all of the equipment and tools, and Mom. And the baby. Let's not forget the baby.

"We cleaned up, paid to replace everything that couldn't be saved, and treated the family to dinner," Matt said. The family forgave them, but Matt swore his team to secrecy and stashed the story deep in his mental vault. He couldn't let it get out that they had *painted a baby*. Who would do business with them if they found out? I mean, what paint company has ever accidentally painted a friggin' baby? Like ever?

Now, Matt found himself sharing all of this with his prospect, the one who wanted to know about the really bad stuff. He ended up signing the contract because Matt had told him the worst mistake his company had ever made, and more importantly, *how they handled it.* By showing how M & E Painting made it right with the family in Windsor, Colorado, his new customer understood that if the company also made a mistake on his job, M & E would rectify it. Matt's secret was out, and it wasn't the end of the world. He didn't die. In fact, he scored a new customer.

Looking at his glossy, happy, we're-so-awesome brochure later that night, Matt got an idea. What if he didn't leave out the bad stuff? What if he came clean about the painted baby story?

"I'd always kept my ear to the ground to make sure my secret was under lock and key, terrified it would get out," Matt told me. "Then I realized, no company is perfect, and I should stop trying to make ours the exception. Customers are looking for our potential flaws and what could potentially go wrong if they were to work with us. Why not show them what *could* go wrong and how we'd handle it?"

Matt went for it. He changed his brochures, his advertising, all of it, to include the "painted baby story." The response he received from professional advertisers was not great, to say the least.

"The first time I openly shared our new method of marketing to an advertising vendor we worked closely with, he said, 'That is the stupidest, most ridiculous, career-damaging thing you could ever do, Matt. That is company suicide and I want nothing to do with it. You are flat-out crazy.' I knew the painted baby story would piss some people off. It was so against the norm—no one would have the guts to attempt it. But I still didn't expect my marketing partners to have such a strong negative response."

This wasn't the first time Matt tried something no one else would do. It was a huge risk, but he went for it and implemented his "crazy" idea. You know what happened? Good stuff, that's what. His marketing passed the blink test. His sales, close ratios, profitability, and buzz about the company exploded. His idea was so different, so out there, it got the attention of people other than those his standard-issue brochure and advertising ever did. And, because he told that painted baby story from the heart, because it authentically reflected his company's values, it attracted his ideal customers, who were ready to follow his directive and call him for a quote. The ever-so-popular "business transparency" movement you hear about today was started years back by some guy making a baby opaque.

So ask yourself, what have you messed up? What can't you do? What costs way too much? What do you do that may unintentionally make your customer's life harder? Any one of those things can be your disadvantage advantage.

Among other aspects of human nature, award-winning American psychologist Elliot Aronson studied the effects of "blunder" on likability. He is the first to describe the pratfall effect, which proved that people have a tendency to like a person more after they make an everyday mistake. In marketing, this is sometimes called the blemishing effect. Whatever you want to call it, it works.

We like actors more once we've seen their blooper reels. We are more apt to trust a politician who admits they were wrong. We are more drawn to the underdogs who tripped and fell but got back up and finished the race. I'm no scientist—though my smoker grill may beg to differ—but it's my guess that people who make mistakes are more appealing simply because they are more relatable. They appear just like us—flawed, fallible, and can't throw a football. (Okay, that last one is just me.)

"We are all humans, and we all make mistakes at times," Matt told me. "I now believe that a company truly shines and shows its moral fiber when things don't go as planned. Within my painting company, we take just as much ownership, accountability, and responsibility for our mistakes and imperfections as we do our excellent projects and fantastic reviews. Everybody has a 'painted baby' story, but not everybody will take ownership of that story and use the story as an example of how they step up and serve their customers and their community. That's why it is your advantage."

Share what your competition is afraid to share: the truth.

The Gift of Weirdness

Michalowicz. That is a doooozy of a last name. Other words with that many syllables include "conjubilant," "taradiddle," and "collywobbles." I have no idea what any of those words mean. (Yes, they are real words.) My last name falls in that same category. Most people mispronounce it, which includes me, apparently, because I was once corrected by a Ukrainian gentleman who said it is not "Mi-cow-low-wits" but "Me-ha-low-vitch." And spelling it, well forget it. Everyone struggles, including a few relatives. (I am talking to you, cousin Peter Mycallowicks.) Remember, your weakness is your strength.

No surprise, I leaned in. I make fun of my name before anyone else can, not because it bothers me when people call me "Michal-o-shits," but because I know that it's different and it gets noticed. It breaks barriers when you lean into your "weakness," and in this case, makes Stodgy Author Guy seem more approachable. "He's no Stephen King, but he is the biggest 'My-cow-shits' I know," my wife whispered to me when I signed this book deal.

I'm weird in a lot of ways. We all are. Thank God, actually. Why fight it? In fact, being *more* you is probably your greatest marketing advantage.

When I was "too skinny" in grade school, classmates made fun of me. When readers gave me a hard time about my obsession with wearing vests to speaking events, I wrote a story about how I would wear them until the end of time. Then my team made "Live your vest life!" and "Do your very vest!" T-shirts to wear and give to readers. I used to run my business out of an empty office in a cookie factory—above the ovens, no less. That's pretty weird, and some people wouldn't admit to that—especially a business author. "What the heck are you doing there, Mike? Why don't you rent out a cabin for a month and write as you stare at Walden Pond in the distance? Or, I don't know, just use a normal office?" But I didn't hide my digs. I made sure everyone knew about it. I was up there writing *The Pumpkin Plan*, sweat pouring down my face. Not because of the pressure alone, but because my office had no air-conditioning or windows and reached ninety-eight degrees on hot days. I called it my "death by chocolate chip cookie" office.

Weird isn't bad.

Weird is humanizing.

Weird is a discussion point.

Weird wins the marketing milliseconds.

Weird is *different*, and I believe we have firmly established the fact that different is better.

You have a weirdness, too. Weird is a gift. Embrace it. Share it. Market it.

The Second-Best Leverage

With more than thirty-six thousand franchises in more than one hundred twenty countries, McDonald's kicks Burger King's ass. With fifteen thousand franchises in eighty-four countries, Burger King can't claim to be anything but second best—at least in terms of reach. Instead of trying to grow out of that ranking, Burger King used that to its advantage in an inspired 2018 campaign, the "Whopper Detour."

In a press release, Burger King said it was "turning more than fourteen thousand McDonald's into Burger King restaurants." Here's how Burger King did it. The company offered one-cent Whoppers for a limited time, and to claim that deal, customers would have to install the Burger King app and then stand within six hundred feet of a McDonald's. This unlocked the promotion, allowed customers to place their orders, and then "detoured" them away from McDonald's to the nearest Burger King.

Umm—I think I'm lovin' it. I'm in love with Burger King, or whoever came up with that crazy, stick-it-to-the-big-guys idea. I love how it leverages the strength of the biggest competitor, just as David used Goliath's bigger size to his advantage. Goliath's size made him a slower adversary, allowing David to relentlessly wing rocks at his face. David could hit him with a stone and run to a new location for the next stone throw. In this way, Goliath's "strength" made him the perfect target.

Burger King used the sheer number of McDonald's locations to its advantage. Those BILLIONS SERVED billboards at the McDonald's restaurants? Burger King changed them, in their marketing, to read BILLIONS SWERVED. The nine-day campaign yielded remarkable results:[2] The Burger King app was downloaded more than one and a half million times, and the company had a 300 percent increase in mobile app revenue. It also got Burger King a lot of attention. *The New York Times, USA Today, Business Insider* and major television networks such as CNN and MSNBC covered its different marketing experiment. Burger King also had an 818 percent increase in Twitter mentions.

If you're second best or, even better, way down the list in your industry, consider how you can use that ranking to your advantage. Instead of hiding it, how could you play it up? How can you leverage the strength of your competition to make *you* stronger?

The Opportunity of Lack

If you're just starting out in business, you may not want people to know what you don't have. It's normal to want to appear like everyone else in your industry, like a legit company with all the bells and whistles. So we buy all the things that other people seem to have, once again trying to fit in. I did it, for a while, until I figured out that it was all bullshit. I thought I had to have the expensive equipment and gear to show my company's technical capabilities when prospects would come to visit the offices of my first computer service company. Fancy gear piled up, adding zero value to my services, and it never managed to impress prospects. Twenty dollars' worth of blinking Christmas tree lights in a server cabinet would have been more impressive, and more effective marketing, than the twenty thousand I racked up on credit cards that impressed no one.*

Not having the money to pay for something everyone else has can actually be the greatest opportunity to differentiate. When Jesse and Emily Cole took over what would become the Savannah Bananas, the historic Grayson Stadium had an electric scoreboard. Then that scoreboard was hit by lighting. It couldn't be repaired and they didn't have the funds to replace it. So, they went with the old manual scoreboard. You know, the kind that requires a person to sit behind it during the game and change the metal numbers by hand? Now their hand-operated scoreboard

---

* If you and I run into each other at some point, ask me about the blinking Christmas lights in server cabinets. I will share how it made for some of the best and most different marketing I have ever done. The result? That company was acquired by a Fortune 500.

has become a marketing tool. It adds to the vibe during the game, and the press has written entire articles just about the old-timey scoreboard. Instead of being a ballpark that doesn't have an electric scoreboard, Grayson Stadium is now one of the few ballparks in the country that *still has* a manual scoreboard. Besides, Jesse soon discovered most people weren't even paying attention to the score, so why bother replacing it with the usual (ignorable) stuff that would cost a fortune?

What are you saving up to buy for your business? What's something you *think* your customers expect you to have that you can't afford? That thing you don't have could actually be a feature, not a flaw.

~~~~

Dolly Parton is inarguably one of the greatest American songwriters. She's written dozens of hits, has more awards than I can count, and even has her own theme park. I mean, how many celebrities have their own theme park? She's a musical genius, an icon, and a damn good businessperson. And yet, when you think of Dolly, you probably also think of the way she looks. Big blond hair. "Gaudy" (her word, not mine) clothes and lots of makeup. She's also known for her, well, uh, let me say, "figure."

Barbara Walters once asked her in an interview, "Why do you dress the way you do?"

Dolly replied, "To shock. To be different."

Early on in her career, the suits wanted Dolly to change her look. They urged her to tone it down, to change her hair color, to look more like her contemporaries. She knew that was horrible advice. Why would she want to look like everyone else? Not only did she ignore their advice and lean even further into her look, her first single poked fun at what some people perceived as her disadvantage. Released in 1966, "Dumb Blonde" asserted her power and turned the stereotype about blonds on its ass. It was a supersmart move on her part, because she leaned into the thing that people gave her a hard time about, the thing that people wanted her to change. It was the first step in differentiating herself, and in doing so, finding her fans.

You're going to make fun of my hair, I'll make it taller.

You're going to make fun of my boobs, I'll put them front and center.

You're going to make fun of my fashion, I'll kick it up ten notches.

In an interview for *USA Today,* she once said, "The whole magic about me is that I look artificial, but I'm totally real."

Dolly knows what's up. She has one of the most dedicated and diverse fan bases in the world—maybe *the* most. She also has one of the highest positive Q scores[3] in the world. Owned by Marketing Evaluations, Inc., the Q score tracks the public awareness and appeal of a celebrity. In essence—it's tracking the first two letters in the DAD Marketing Framework—Differentiate and Attract. If a celebrity has a high Q score, they are more highly regarded, and as a result they command more bucks for promoting products and services.

You can attract a dedicated and diverse customer base, too.

Don't hide who you are, what you don't have, or the mistakes you've made. Let your freak flag fly.

Your Turn

My favorite quote, often attributed to author Oscar Wilde hangs in my office. He said, "Be yourself. Everyone else is already taken." Bingo flamingo! That's it. That thing you want to hide, that people shame you over, that is the skeleton in your closet. That thing could be your marketing liberation.

1. If you are marketing for your own business, ask yourself how you can put your weakness, your weirdness, your "I ain't gonna hide it anymore" differentness front and center.

2. If you work in the marketing department, this is your moment. What is the weird story that is in the annals of the company's history? What is the weirdness that everyone in the office loves but avoids putting out there to keep the professionalism up? What is the biggest thing your competition picks on? That is your opportunity. Be the bold marketer that brings that front and center.

CHAPTER TEN

Reimagine Your Business

L ife is good on the South Dakota plains, especially when you've figured out how to earn enough revenue to support the lifestyle you envision. With two brick-and-mortar locations and a roasting facility, Jacob Limmer had grown his Cottonwood Coffee from a side hustle to a business anyone would be proud to own.

You might remember Jacob's story from *Fix This Next*. In that book, I give you a simple system to figure out which aspect of your business to focus on first in order to achieve consistent, permanent growth. By following that system, Jacob discovered that his company did not generate enough to support what he called his "Midwest comfort" lifestyle. After thirteen years in business, trying to sell more and more, this came as a shock to him. So, he went right back to basics—profitable sales, not more sales. By making this shift, Jacob soon had more than enough income to support all he needed and wanted. Once again, life was good on the South Dakota plains.

Then, in the spring of 2020, his sales all but dried up. As was the case for so many storefront businesses, when COVID-19 forced many Americans to stay home, Jacob had to temporarily close both of his coffee shops. At this point, he had two choices: he could wait things out and hope for better days, or he could rise to the occasion and *create* better days.

Jacob chose option two.

Weeks into a global pandemic, he knew that simply switching up the marketing would not be enough to keep the sales flowing. So he surveyed his clients. He sent them emails that said, and I'm paraphrasing here: "How are you feeling? What do you need? We're still open for business but realize we need to serve you in a new way. What can we do for you now?"

Through that survey, Jacob learned that his clients were concerned about health, and that they wanted to be uplifted. His clients also noted that they missed the ritual of getting a delicious Cottonwood Coffee drink.

Within twenty-two days of shuttering his two locations, Jacob had created a new product, an immune-booster cold brew infused with high-quality vitamin D3, added it to the online store, and let his clients know about the new product. Sales went up and allowed Cottonwood Coffee to weather the COVID-19 shutdowns long enough to reopen its stores. And, even though their revenue was down for the year, Cottonwood Coffee had its most profitable year ever. That, though, is not the end of the story. During those first months of the pandemic, Jacob learned something he couldn't have seen before: How to reimagine his business.

On a catch-up call, Jacob told me, "I feel more in control than I ever have before. I know now that I don't have to sacrifice my life to support my business, ever again. I can adapt to whatever happens and whatever I need by reimagining it."

The day may come when no matter how different your marketing is, no matter how many times you experiment-improve-experiment, and no matter how buff your marketing muscle has become, you can't sell enough of your thing. It happens to all of us. Tides turn. Tastes change. Disruption happens. Copycats emerge.

As business owners, we have to face these realities and come to terms with the fact that sometimes no amount of marketing—no matter how brilliant—is enough. When this happens, we have two choices: we can wait things out and hope for better days, or we can rise to the occasion and *create* better days. To do that, we have to reimagine our businesses—our offers, how we market them, even who our customer base should be. We have to be willing to shift the *way* we do business, not just how we market.

You, my friend, are now more equipped to handle these business detours because you've practiced getting different. You're getting more comfortable coloring outside of the lines. You've become more confident standing out. You've got this.

Jacob Limmer created a new product in order to weather a rough storm. He did that by reaching out to his peeps to find out what they needed, and then tested their feedback with their wallets. That approach is a no-brainer, and super easy to implement. In this chapter, you'll learn more simple but powerful strategies you can use to differentiate *what* you offer not just *how* you offer it, so you too can reimagine, and maybe even reinvent, your business.

Take One Step Back

In 2020, I talked with a lot of business owners who, like Jacob, had to figure out a way to stay afloat. Fortunately, many of my *Profit First* readers had banked months of operating expenses, and so they had time—a runway of cash allowed them to keep their doors open and their people gainfully employed. Still, they needed revenue, and for many of them, that meant rethinking everything.

Unsurprisingly, I also consulted with a lot of restaurant owners that year. To help them reimagine their business, I shared my 1-Step Back Method.

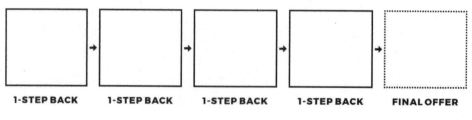

1-STEP BACK   1-STEP BACK   1-STEP BACK   1-STEP BACK   FINAL OFFER

1-Step Back Method

It works like this:

1. Look at your historical offering, the main thing you do. So, for most restaurants, that's feeding people at their

location. Write your deliverable in the FINAL OFFER box. For this example, it would be "put good food on the table" or similar.

2. Then, record the last step that you take immediately prior to delivering the FINAL OFFER. This one is easy for restaurants: Before a server puts food on a diner's table, they carry it there from the kitchen. That's one step back. Put "carry food to table" in the 1-STEP BACK box immediately to the left of the FINAL OFFER.

3. Now, consider how you could change your offer based on that step. This is what many restaurants did in 2020— carrying food to a table became carrying food out of the restaurant in the form of takeout and delivery. Many of them were not adequately set up for this, but they sure are now! And this simple shift saved a lot of brick-and-mortar businesses from going under, including retail stores and even bars. Who knew that "takeout margaritas" were so good? Everybody. That's who.

4. Here's where it gets interesting. Take one *more* step back. What happens before that prior step? For restaurants, that's cooking the meal in the kitchen. Put that in the next left 1-STEP BACK box. Then consider how this could become a new offering, such as cooking a meal in the home kitchen. I coached Mariana Oviedo, a business owner in Ensenada, Mexico, to do exactly that via virtual cooking classes. These classes allowed her patrons

to feel connected with other members of their community and eat the food they loved. For this, Maria charged one hundred fifty dollars, which included delivery of all the ingredients students needed for the class. Before the lockdowns, a typical reservation yielded about fifty dollars. Now, she was positioned to bring in three times that amount, simply by taking one step back, and then another. What is *your* next step back? Put that in the box.

5. Keep rewinding step-by-step until you have identified all the significant steps you take to get to your historical offer. For restaurants, the step before cooking the meal in the kitchen is taking the order. In my community here in New Jersey, one restaurant changed the way it offered takeout and delivery. It eliminated the traditional "place your order" step, which required waiting thirty to sixty minutes for your meal. Instead, it partnered with a food truck in the area to deliver meals, one neighborhood at a time. The restaurant loaded up the truck with sixty prepared meals and parked it in a cul-de-sac—sort of like an ice cream truck. Genius, right?

Once you've zeroed in on the one step you want to differentiate, play with the idea to make variations of it. Then, run a beta. If it works out, amplify it. As you know by now, the key to successfully doing different is to keep at it. Brainstorm, think it through, try and try again. And, as always, listen to the wallets, not the words.

Sell the Tell

One sure way to figure out whether your offer will get traction is to sell it before you create it. Sell the Tell, not the thing—yet. If people want to buy your thing just on concept, that means you have an idea that is worth development. That means they believe in it and can envision it working for them. If no one buys it, there's your answer. At that point you either improve on the offer or ditch it and try something new.

Here's how it works:

1.   Share details on your idea with your community. This could be through email, on social media, or even in person. This is not an official offer or pitch. Shocker of shocks, integrity wins here. Tell them you have an idea, and the key components you intend to include.

2.   Inoculate them to the inevitable bumps and bruises. Be up front about the fact that you have a new idea you want to try and that, because it's new, you may make mistakes and it will surely need improvements.

3.   Then ask your community if they want your thing. Do they think the idea is useful? Do they need it? Remember, we want to focus on wallets, not words. So ask for a deposit. The Direct part here should be based on a discounted price, and you should remind people that this is a beta concept,

hence the potential for tweaks and edits, and hence the discount.

4. Send out the request within twenty-four hours of thinking it up. This is a lesson from our friend Jesse Cole. Have the idea, put the basic bullet points to it, determine the ultimate price, discount it for the people willing to get it early and rough, and get them to commit with cash.

5. If you *don't* get enough positive responses (deposits), seek feedback on what needs to change and then try again. Or set it aside and move on to the next idea.

6. Involve your beta customers in improving your thing. Ask for their feedback and make changes quickly as you deliver the first version of this next offering. Cater to them so that your wobbly, "not quite ready for prime time" idea evolves into a solid, effective offer.

7. After you've finished your beta, roll it out at full price. The beauty of this is, because you (eventually) delivered it to your beta customers while actively taking and acting upon their feedack, they will rave about it. Now you'll have your pick of testimonials to help you sell this new thing.

I've seen far too many business owners flesh out their idea, build it, and test it before they approach their ideal customers to see if they even want it. Two very frustrating results come from this approach. First, they may have created something few people actually want or need. Secondly, development and rollout take way too long and the opportunity may pass by. In the end, that's wasted money and wasted time. When we create offers in a bubble, cut off from our communities, we rely on a data set of one (ourselves) and may end up developing an offer the market doesn't want. But when you Sell the Tell, you know for sure that people will buy your thing *and* that confirmation lights a fire under you to make it happen.

Ask, "Who Else Benefits?"

The Relentless Redhead would not let COVID-19 win. In March of 2020, just thirty-six days before her annual IT Sales and Marketing Boot Camp, Robin Robins had to shut down the live event and pivot to virtual. Now, this may sound like a doable, if tough, challenge. In reality, it was a *massive* undertaking. By now, we've all grown used to virtual events, but in March, it seemed almost unthinkable. I say this from personal experience. I also had an event in March that had to pivot to virtual in less than three weeks—AuthorUpLive—and we had no idea how to pull it off without refunding most of our registrations. It required immediate technology changes, and minute-by-minute learning for hosts. And for the guests?

Few people had confidence in virtual events, especially one that was as much about in-person networking as it was about learning. To top it off, most people were not Zoom savvy, including, apparently, CNN host Jeffrey Toobin, who was caught, um, playing with his *tube in* a Zoom session for work. If you don't know what I am talking about, don't do a web search for it . . . you'll go blind.

The Relentless Redhead Robin would not be deterred. And she didn't follow the status quo. When everyone else—including me—shifted events to Zoom, she hired a TV production crew, built a physical stage for live presentations from speakers, and added screens with live feeds to show all of the people tuning in from their homes. Although they had to refund more than six hundred and fifty thousand dollars in the first thirty days (attributed to panicked sponsors mostly), Robin more than made up for that by increasing her registration list from fifteen hundred to nearly five thousand! In six weeks. Where everyone else—again, including me—just tried to hang on to their attendees, Robin grew that list by leaps and bounds, found new sponsors, and netted her most profitable event ever.

Robin's reputation for world-class events quickly evolved into a reputation for world-class virtual events. When I interviewed her for this book in the fall of 2020, Robin told me she had already surpassed $20 million in revenue that year. She also launched Big Red Media, a facilitator of virtual events and marketing services, which grossed $4 million in its first year.

She said, "When things change, it puts everyone back to the opportunity of 'first mover advantage.' You can't afford the time to see what everyone else does."

One of the techniques she uses is to ask, "Who else benefits when

I make a sale?" For an event where the sale is an attendee buying a ticket, the other beneficiaries include the ticket processing company, the virtual event platform, and the production crew. When her in-person events return, she can add food service, hotels, transportation, and more. Robin sees all of these people and companies who benefit as opportunities for vendor alliances, joint ventures, partnerships, and sponsorships. Which of these vendors also want to serve Robin's clients? Which of these vendors have networks of their own that could benefit from Robin's skills? At a gathering of IT professionals, who else wants to access IT professionals?

Because she asked, "Who else benefits?" Robin teamed up with Datto, a data backup company that wanted access to her attendees and paid a pretty sum for it. She then asked, "How *else* can they benefit?" Turns out, they had a massive prospect list but didn't know how to leverage it. Robin then created and ran a virtual conference for Datto. She now has a division of her business that runs virtual conferences for other companies.

To reimagine or even reinvent your business, ask yourself, "Who else benefits?" Keep asking it until you find new opportunities.

Do What *Doesn't* Scale

One of my favorite books is Joey Coleman's *Never Lose a Customer Again*. It is a must-read. May I be so bold as to suggest that it is the perfect one-two punch with this book. *Get Different* will help you land customers, and Joey's book will help you keep them.

I invited Joey to a gathering of fellow authors, and that's when he shared one of his best methods for getting different. It was his advice that inspired me to create the immersive learning experience for this book—immersewithmike.com. And it was this gem of a statement that really blew my mind:

"Do what doesn't scale, because no one else will do it."

When he said that, I thought, "My God, that's raw brilliance!" Of course that's the secret to reimagining your offer, because most people want to scale and avoid doing things that can't be replicated easily. Creating something that won't scale puts too much demand on them and they eventually burn out.

That was a "duh, why didn't I think of that?" moment for me, and I ran with it. I started to think about how I engaged with readers. Most authors don't engage one-on-one with their readers because they can't scale it. I get it—they can't have a personal connection with everyone who consumes their books. It's not possible, and even if it were, it would be too draining.

Before Joey shared the unscalable strategy with me, I had already been responding to emails from readers, personally. It's important to me to connect with them—and with *you*. The problem was, I couldn't keep up with the demand. I decided I had to give it up. All authors have to hand things off to their teams eventually, right? Except, deep down, I really didn't want to lose that connection with you.

So, after that author gathering, I recommitted to reader engagement and challenged myself to find a way to make it work. I developed systems and implemented time blocking so I can respond to all of the reader emails I receive. The response has been amazing. How I handle this is "secret sauce" stuff, but I do type every single word and record every single video. It's me and it's "not" scalable. Or is it?

Try this technique. Kick it around for an hour or so. Ask yourself, "What if?" What if you weren't concerned about scalability? What if the inability to scale something was just an industry myth, and you can in fact grow it? What would you offer? Or how would you deliver your offer differently? What if you simply did what can't be scaled in your industry and filled the gap with raw effort? That just might be your secret sauce.

〰〰〰

John Ruhlin has sold more knives than any other salesperson in Cutco history, and he did it by changing the *way* he sold them. Cutco sells knives primarily through direct sales, the good old-fashioned door-to-door method. When John was an intern, he had an idea. What if he could get business owners to purchase large quantities of knives to give as gifts to their clients?

His first sale of this nature was to his girlfriend's father, an attorney, who bought pocketknives as gifts for his clients. That was just the beginning. He would go on to sell more than $4 million worth of Cutco knives.

John is a friend. He is also the author of *Giftology: The Art and Science of Using Gifts to Cut through the Noise, Increase Referrals, and Strengthen Retention.* His different approach to selling not only worked for Cutco but also became John's life's work.

The key to succeeding at marketing and sales is to continually ask yourself, "What if I tried a different way? What if I tried a different sales approach? What if I borrowed a product or service delivery system from a completely different industry? What if I bucked conventional wisdom, set aside industry norms, and tried something completely out of the box?" When you reimagine the big stuff—what you sell and how you sell it—you just might discover your true calling.

Your Turn

1. Ask yourself who else benefits from the product or services you provide. Beyond your customers, there are vendors, suppliers, contractors, and others in the food chain. Document all the other people who participate in the creation or delivery of what you do. They are beneficiaries. Now ask yourself, "How else can they be partners?"

2. Create a list of all the things in your industry that "can't be scaled." Ask yourself what the industry doesn't do because people say it can't be done. Then pick one and actually do it. If you did the book immersion I put in the dedication, share your story of how you used Get Different for your business. This is a win-win. I am always looking for new stories and strategies (that serves me, thank you) and it may turn into a blog or podcast mention or inclusion in one of my future books (that, I hope, is a win for you). If you didn't do the immersion, you still can! Just go to immersewithmike.com.

Grow, but Don't Grow Up

G row up." At this point, you know me well enough to figure out that I'm not a fan of that phrase. I am fifty years old now (I know, I know, I don't look a day over forty-nine and a half), and I've been told that more times than I can count—and as recently as last week. Maybe because I'm a goofball. Maybe because I'm not afraid to try different stuff. Maybe because I have a childlike enthusiasm for the things I love.

I'm no Peter Pan. I like being a grown-up, married dad of three.

My businesses, though? They are a different story. I definitely don't want my companies to grow up, because that's code for "fit in with the rest of the world."

As we grow into adults, we start to comply more and more

with society around us. We take fewer risks. We want to belong. "Grow up" becomes code for "fall in line, bucko. Color inside the lines. Conform."

Do. What. Is. Expected.

No thanks.

It's the business owners who don't grow up who stand out. The leaders who don't fit in. Those kids who don't color within the lines, or just make their own new lines. Those kids who don't dress like you are supposed to dress. The kids who have unique points of view.

According to News Medical, Steve Jobs had koumpounopho-bia, the fear of buttons. At the very least, he had a strong aversion to buttons. Jobs always wore a turtleneck. No buttons. And his jeans? They surely weren't button flies. Instead of forcing himself to comply with buttons, he rejected them. And that rejection carried through to the products he developed.

When Apple launched the iPhone it revolutionized the phone industry. The dominant player in the market at the time was BlackBerry. If you had a cell phone, chances are it was the "Crack-Berry." Competing phones tried to pack in more buttons, because that was the industry norm, as defined by BlackBerry. Companies put entire keyboards behind screens that you could slide up with your thumb and type away. But Steve Jobs stayed true to himself. No buttons. When the iPhone released on January 9, 2007, Apple was the first major company to reinvent the design to be buttonless. It blended technology with art. Ten years later, in the fourth quarter of 2016, BlackBerry dropped to 0.0 market share. Stick a fork in BlackBerry, they're done. Apple became the dominant player.

Different wins when reinventing business and reinventing marketing. The wonderful thing is different doesn't require *you* to be different. Different requires you to be you, full out. We all are different. But only the people who fully embrace who they are and express it are noticed. Don't grow up. I beg of you.

I am not saying be childish, unless that is who you truly are. I am saying embrace that inner child. Lean into who you always were and still are.

I want my businesses to grow, not grow up. If I let my businesses comply with all things "expected," we'll lose our ability to stand out in the marketplace. And in turn, we'll lose our ability to expand and increase revenues. That's the great irony. We strive for our businesses to be like any other legit business and we end up stunting our own growth by trying to be "legit."

Not you, though. You know what's up. You now understand why doing different is the essential key to getting noticed. And you know that *your* different could be super simple, a small tweak to the "standard operating procedure." And you now have a proven framework to evaluate and experiment with your different marketing ideas. Now, in an instant, you can look at any marketing—yours, your competition's, someone trying to market to you—and know if it has a shot at working or not. If it fails the DAD test, it fails. It's that simple.

For marketing to work, as it always has been and always will be, it must Differentiate, Attract, and Direct explicitly. Do it and you win. Don't and you are just more background noise.

You've already started working your marketing muscle. You may have come into this book with a fear of marketing or, at the very least, a feeling that you just didn't have what it takes to come up with out-of-the-box ideas. Now, you know that's bunk. Your marketing muscles are getting stronger with every Get Different Experiment. And as you try new approaches and roll out the ideas that worked, your confidence will grow right along with your business. You'll be far less concerned about *what* other people think, and far more concerned with *how* the right people think—and what makes them take notice, desire, and act.

You'll be better able to calculate risk and take chances you may not have taken in the past. You'll have that swagger that only comes from knowing that you have taken control of your business growth. You can turn the dial up or down, at will. The flow of leads is entirely up to you.

When people tell me and you to "grow up," sometimes the motive behind that is to get us to accept a reality that doesn't align with our values. Why would we want to do that? I'm on a mission to eradicate entrepreneurial poverty. You are on a mission, too. We can't accept anything as the "status quo." This may upset some people, but we have to be true to who we are.

And sometimes, just sometimes, when people tell us to "grow up" it's because *they* are afraid. They may realize they have lost connection with their true selves. Or they may have a sense that they are living their lives in fear, as opposed to expression. These people want you to "grow up" so that you comply with them. They want you to stop being noticed so that they don't feel bad about not being noticed themselves.

Marketing doesn't just happen in business. It happens with not-for-profits, in politics, and on school grounds. And some different "marketing" missions take a long time, but that doesn't mean they're not worth doing. At a game in the 2016 football season, San Francisco 49er Colin Kaepernick took a knee during the national anthem rather than stand with his hand over heart, as is tradition. *That* was different. He got the idea from a veteran who explained that is a military tradition to take a knee at the grave of a fallen soldier. There is symmetry there, as it is common in youth sports leagues for players to take a knee when one of their teammates is injured on the field. Kaepernick reasoned that this would be different enough to get the attention of the nation to an important issue that he felt was being overlooked, and it honored the "fallen" men and women who lost their lives to police brutality. His "marketing" goal was awareness. His "don't grow up" method was a sobering, very "grown-up" resistance to conformity.

Except it didn't go down as he'd hoped. He was vilified by many fans, NFL team owners, politicians. The NFL banned kneeling during the national anthem, and by 2017, the 49ers released Kaepernick from the team. It wasn't until 2020, after the death of George Floyd, that the NFL retracted their earlier statements. NFL commissioner Roger Goodell said, "We, the National Football League, admit we were wrong for not listening to the NFL players earlier and encourage all to speak out and peacefully protest." Some might argue that, because Kaepernick has not yet been assigned to a team since 2016, it wasn't worth it, that his efforts didn't work. I would argue that they *did* work. His different strategy ultimately showed the power of peaceful protest. It was different from what everyone else did, so it got noticed. Different always wins. If you know it's right, stick with it. Relentlessly.

Don't give in to the sea of sameness. Don't give in to the trendy thing, the best practices, the industry standards, or the "everyone does it" justification. You know the key to marketing is to win the blink, and different will get you where you need to go.

Don't give up on your mission. Don't sell out. Don't give up on the growth you want to see for your business. Don't give up on your dreams. Use Get Different marketing to help you get there.

When my son Jake applied to my beloved alma mater, Virginia Tech, he got waitlisted. That's like furloughing someone as opposed to firing them—but before they even start the job. Jake didn't accept that decision. He knew he was one of a sea of applicants, and decided to do something different that would get the attention of the admissions department. Jake created a massive poster board that showed all of the reasons why he should be accepted, and mailed it to Virginia Tech.

Shortly after, he received a phone call from the dean of admissions. "In my twenty-five years in this job, I've never received a poster board like that. We can't promise anything, but we need to reevaluate our consideration." *We need to reevaluate our consideration.* Different worked. Different always wins.*

If you believe in yourself and your business, stick with it. If you believe you are the best solution, if you know you are the best solution, you must stick with it. You must stand out. You have a responsibility to get noticed. It is the first and necessary step to be of service.

When I was in Berlin, I got a fortune cookie message that read "Be bold, *be italic,* but never be regular." I keep it with me as a

---

* Jake ultimately chose to go to Rutgers. Jake's "marketing" put him in the driver's seat. He picked a school that he loves. Jake won. Rutgers won. And I feel VT lost. Sorry, Tech.

reminder to continue practicing being different, to keep working that marketing muscle, to keep trying to master the marketing milliseconds. We all need the reminder, because the pull to fit in is strong and has the allure of being easier. Being different is the bold (and *italic*) amplification of your own idiosyncrasies, of your authentic self. That's why it is always better, and that's why it always wins.

If I could insert my own message into fortune cookies all over the world, if I could ensure that it would land on your plate after dinner, it would read: "Let your business grow, not grow up." Take what you've learned in this book and dream a bigger dream. Now that you know how to get noticed by the right people, the sky's the limit.

What could you do if you knew for sure that you could get all of the leads you needed when you needed them? What if you could surpass reasonable expectations, just skate right on by them, off into the stratosphere of possibilities? What would you do then? What would you create? What would you innovate? How would you serve?

You're no longer at the base of the mountain trying to figure out the best path to the top. In reading this book and trying your own Get Different Experiments, in committing to being *authentically* different, you're already there. You're at the summit, and the view is different from up here. You can see for miles. What's on the horizon for your business?

Whatever it is, I know you've got this. You're different, and I for one like that. A lot.

So how about it? Are you ready to get different?

It's your turn.

Appendix I 〉

The Get Different Marketing Process guides you through experiments, variable modifications, and ultimately rolling out a successful experiment into a marketing plan.

GD MARKETING PROCESS

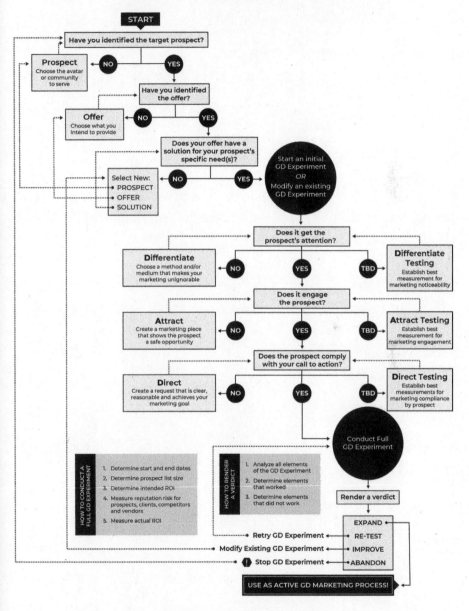

The Get Different Marketing Process

Appendix II ⟩

The Expanded DAD Marketing Framework shows the stages of millisecond marketing. You first must Differentiate to get the prospect's attention. This moment lasts for about one-tenth of a second, faster than it takes to blink. Then you must Attract the prospect to keep them engaged. You must show and continue to show the prospect that the opportunity afforded by paying attention outweighs abandoning your marketing. You will only keep a prospect engaged as long as they derive value and see an opportunity. In the final stage, you Direct the prospect to take action. For them to be compelled they must see that the opportunity of complying with your request outweighs the risk.

	DIFFERENTIATE	**ATTRACT**	**DIRECT**
MARKETING OBJECTIVE	Prospect Attention	Prospect Engagement	Prospect Compliance
DECISION SPEED	1/10th of a second	Accumulating 1/4 second increments	1/4 second
FAILURE POINTS	Known Threat = Avoid Known Irrelevant = Ignore	New Threat = Avoid New Irrelevant = Ignore	Unreasonable Ask = Avoid
SUCCESS POINTS	Known Opportunity = Prospect Engagement or Unknown & Unexpected = Prospect Engagement	New Opportunity = Prospect Consideration	Reasonble Ask = Prospect Compliance

The Expanded DAD Marketing Framework

Appendix III ⟩

The Get Different Experiment Sheet. Run every marketing experiment using this tool, and then render a verdict. When you have identified an Expand & Track marketing experiment, you have found something to roll out into your marketing plan.

GD EXPERIMENT SHEET

FOR _____

DATE _____ TEST # _____

STEP 1: OBJECTIVE

WHO
Who is the ideal prospect?

_____

WHAT
What offer serves them best?

_____

WIN
What is the outcome you want?

STEP 2: INVESTMENT

CUSTOMER LTV: _____
The typical life-time value (revenue) of a customer.

CLOSE RATE ODDS: _____ **OF EVERY** _____
Your expected close rate of engaged prospects *e.g. 1 of every 5.*

INVESTMENT PER PROSPECT: _____
The dollar amount you are willing to risk to land a prospect.

NOTES:

STEP 3: EXPERIMENT

MEDIUM: _____
What marketing platform you will use? *e.g. website, email, direct mail, billboard, etc.*

IDEA:

DOES THIS COMPLY WITH THE DAD FRAMEWORK?

❑ **DIFFERENTIATE**
Is it unignorable?

❑ **ATTRACT**
Is it a safe opportunity?

❑ **DIRECT**
Is it a specific and reasonable ask?

STEP 4: MEASUREMENT

INTENTIONS	OUTCOMES
START DATE: _____	**END DATE:** _____
INTENDED # OF PROSPECTS: _____	**ACTUAL # OF PROSPECTS:** _____
INTENDED RETURN: _____	**ACTUAL RETURN:** _____
INTENDED INVESTMENT: _____	**ACTUAL INVESTMENT:** _____

OBSERVATIONS:

VERDICT {

EXPAND & TRACK	RE-TEST	IMPROVE	ABANDON
Use as ongoing strategy	Test new sample	Fix and retry	Start new experiment

The Get Different Experiment Sheet

Appendix IV ⟩

This is a tool to help you refine what makes you (or your organization) different in the eyes of your clients and contacts.

FIND **YOUR** DIFFERENT

NAME _____

DATE _____

STEP 1: FIND THEM

RELATIONSHIPS / CONTACTS:

0-1 YEAR	1-10 YEARS	10+ YEARS
1.	5.	9.
2.	6.	10.
3.	7.	11.
4.	8.	12.

INSTRUCTION: Identify twelve people who know you (or your company) well. Four of the people should be new relationships of under one year. The next four should be people who have known you (or your company) for over one year and less than ten. And the last group of four people are people who have known you (or your company) for ten years or more. You don't need to be in active communication or relationships with these individuals. You do need to have a way to contact them.

STEP 2: ASK THEM

SEND THEM THIS MESSAGE:

My business coach gave me an assignment I need to complete immediately. I am required to pick someone who knows me well, so I would love your help! I need to know what you feel my "Difference Factor" is: something I do better and/or differently than anyone else. Your response doesn't need to be long. A sentence will do. I will use your insights to improve our business positioning. Thank you so much!

❏ 1 ❏ 2 ❏ 3 ❏ 4 ❏ 5 ❏ 6 ❏ 7 ❏ 8 ❏ 9 ❏ 10 ❏ 11 ❏ 12

INSTRUCTION: Send this message to each of the twelve contacts you have listed above. If you are trying to identify your company's uniqueness instead of your own, change the text to say "I am required to pick someone who knows my company well..." and "I need to know what you see as are our company's difference factor."

STEP 3: RANK IT

RANK THE FEEDBACK:

1	2	3

INSTRUCTION: You need minimally ten responses for this exercise to be effective. Reach out to additional contacts if you didn't reach that threshold. Review the responses you receive from the contacts. Identify the three most common observations made about your Difference Factor. Write them in the boxes above, one observation per box.

STEP 4: REFINE IT

YOUR DIFFERENT:

1. _____

   _____Adjective 1:_____

2. _____

   _____Adjective 2:_____

3. _____

   _____Adjective 3:_____

INSTRUCTION: With the top three Different Factors identified in Step 3, write down the three biggest themes you see in these responses. Give each theme a short phrase and adjective that best exemplifies the theme. In your own words, write how these themes can make you different in how you communicate to prospects.

Find Your Different

Author's Note

Thank you for reading *Get Different*. It is my deepest desire that this book will help you achieve the business (and life) goals you envision. It is an honor to be part of your marketing journey.

I would like to ask a favor of you.

Would you be willing to post an honest review of *Get Different*?

I ask because reviews are the most effective way for fellow business owners, leaders, and professionals to discover the book and determine if it will be of value to them.

A review from you, even a single sentence or two, will achieve just that.

To do it, simply go to the website (or the website for the store) where you bought the book and submit your review.

Again, I seek only your honest feedback.

Thank you for considering this. And thank you for being part of *my* marketing journey.

Mike

Acknowledgments

When I set out to write my first book, I thought it was akin to molding a sculpture from a lump of clay. In reflection, it is more like forming pieces of fine jewelry from blocks of marble (that are the size of a house). Precision and perfection are required throughout, and stick-to-itiveness is everything.

As we created *Get Different*, I dropped chunks of marble on the ground and then AJ Harper crafted them into perfectly fitted crowns and rings. I truly feel this book is the best of our fourteen-year partnership. I felt that way about our previous work, *Fix This Next*, too. And I felt that way about *Clockwork* before that, and *Profit First* before that. Every book is even better than the prior, in my opinion. That is my definition of an extraordinary partnership. Thank you for your extraordinary artistry and effort, AJ. And thank you, even more, for your extraordinary friendship.

For fifteen years and counting I have worked with another master artist, Liz Dobrinska. The cover of this book is a result of Liz's work. The graphics inside this book, the websites that accompany this book, and every graphic you see or interact with are Liz's work. I want to thank you, Liz, for choosing to work with me day in and day out. I'll be calling you in about fifteen minutes.

Thank you to Noah Schwartzberg, my editor. I can't say enough good things about working with you. I can only assume I'm "different" from some authors, yet you more than put up with my testing and validating of, well, everything; you saw the value in the process. Dozens of covers tested and validated. Countless titles, subtitles, and advanced reader copies all tested and validated. With so much data coupled with endless ideas from AJ and me, you made sure this book served entrepreneurs in the best way possible. And it never, not for a second, lost my voice. Thank you for tying it all together.

I want to thank Justin Wise, my partner in The Different Company,* the service organization behind this book. Your input has been and continues to be excellent. Not only did you give feedback on the book, you were an innovator of the system itself. Thanks for teaching Get Different to entrepreneurs years before the release of this book. This shit works and you proved it!

Behind the scenes there is a whole team working tirelessly to simplify the entrepreneurial journey. Thank you to Kelsey Ayres, our president, for leading our mission to eradicate entrepreneurial poverty. Thank you to Amy Cartelli for doing anything that needs to be done to move us forward. Thank you to Jenna Lorenz for being the voice of our brand. Thank you to Jeremy Smith for keeping the digital world aware of all that is going on, every day.

---

* If you want to ensure you do *Get Different* right, I encourage you to use our coaching and training services at differentcompany.co. Note it is a dot CO and not a dot COM. Dot COMs are too, you know, ordinary.

Thank you to Erin Chazotte for ensuring I am where I need to be exactly when I need to be there. Thank you to Adayla Michalowicz. That little girl with the piggy bank is now a grown woman pursuing a master's degree—and managing reader communications and doing rando Instagram takeovers. And thanks to our newbie, Cordé Reed, for serving our community of experts so they in turn can serve entrepreneurs.

I also want to acknowledge Armando Perez Jr. of Hoosier Security and CCTV Dynamics. Your story is powerful and will find its place in one of my books, I swear. Thanks for letting me interview you again and again. See, you're kinda in this book. Told you so.

Thank you to you. Your work serves the global economy. Your success is the world's.

P.S. Thank you to my agent. Stephen King would be impressed.

Notes

Chapter One: Your Responsibility to Market

1. H. R. Schiffman, *Sensation and Perception: An Integrated Approach* (New York: John Wiley and Sons, Inc., 2001).

Chapter Three: The Target One Hundred

1. Piroska Bisits-Bullen, "How to Choose a Sample Size (for the Statistically Challenged)," Tools4Dev, accessed November 2, 2019, http://www.tools4dev.org/resources/how-to-choose-a-sample-size/.

Chapter Four: Differentiate for Attention

1. Maury Brown, "A Deep Dive into the MLB's Financial Losses for the 2020 Season," *Forbes*, May 18, 2020, https://www.forbes.com/sites/maurybrown/2020/05/18/a-deep-dive-into-mlbs-financial-losses-for-the-2020-season/?sh=444d20da7f6c.

Chapter Five: Attract for Engagement

1. Therese Fessenden, "The Authority Principle," *Nielsen Norman Group*, February 4, 2018, https://www.nngroup.com/articles/authority-principle/.

2. CJ Ng, "Customers Don't Buy from People They Like, They Buy from Those They Trust," Ezinearticles.com, accessed January 23, 2021, https://ezinearticles.com/?Customers-Dont-Buy-From-People-They-Like,-They-Buy-From-Those-They-Trust.

3. Tom Stafford, "How Liars Create the 'Illusion of Truth,'" BBC, October 26, 2016, https://www.bbc.com/future/article/20161026-how-liars-create-the-illusion-of-truth.

4. Elisa Rogers, "The Psychology of Status Purchases: Why We Buy," Thrive Global, May 6, 2019, https://thriveglobal.com/stories/the-psychology-of-status-purchases-why-we-buy/.

5. Zach St. George, "Curiosity Depends on What You Already Know," *Nautilus*, February 25, 2016, https://nautil.us/issue/33/attraction/curiosity-depends-on-what-you-already-know.

6. Dianne Grande, "The Neuroscience of Feeling Safe and Connected," *Psychology Today*, September 24, 2018, https://www.psychologytoday.com/us/blog/in-it-together/201809/the-neuroscience-feeling-safe-and-connected.

7. Sheryl Nance-Nash, "Watch Out for 'Comfort Buying' during Pandemic," *Newsday*, updated May 10, 2020, https://www.newsday.com/business/coronavirus/comfort-buying-pandemic-1.44477117.

8. Joshua Becker, "Understanding the Diderot Effect (and How to Overcome It)," *Becoming Minimalist*, accessed January 23, 2021, https://www.becomingminimalist.com/diderot/.

9. Karyn Hall, "Create a Sense of Belonging," *Psychology Today*, March 24, 2014, https://www.psychologytoday.com/us/blog/pieces-mind/201403/create-sense-belonging.

10. Mahtab Alam Quddusi, "The Importance of Good Health in Our Life—How Can We Achieve Good Health and Well Being?," *The Scientific World*, December 27, 2019, https://www.scientificworld-info.com/2019/12/importance-of-good-health-in-our-life.html.

11. Cole Schafer, "The Psychology of Selling," *Honey Copy*, July 1, 2018, https://www.honeycopy.com/copywritingblog/the-psychology-of-selling.

12. Divya Pahwa, "Why Are We Attracted to Beautiful Things?," *Be Yourself*, August 11, 2013, https://byrslf.co/why-are-we-attracted-to-beautiful-things-b65f0e76074a.

13. "The Need for Recognition, Cornerstone of Self-Esteem," *Exploring Your Mind*, January 18, 2016, https://exploringyourmind.com/need-recognition-cornerstone-self-esteem/.

14. Robert Stephens, "Robert Stephens Founded the Geek Squad and Took It from Bootstrapped Inception to Over $1 Billion in (Estimated) Revenues (Just Watch This Interview. Trust Me. It's Good.)," interview by Clay Collins, *The Marketing Show*, Leadpages (transcript), July 10, 2012, https://www.leadpages.com/blog/robert-stephens-geek-squad-best-buy/.

Chapter Six: Direct for Results

1. W. Michael Lynn, *MegaTips 2: Twenty Tested Techniques to Increase Your Tips*, *Cornell Hospitality Tools* 2, no. 1 (March 2011), https://static.secure.website/wscfus/5261551/uploads/CHRmegatips2.pdf.

Chapter Nine: The Disadvantage Advantage

1. Anne Raver, "Now It Can Be Told: All about Squirrels and Nuts," *New York Times*, December 11, 1994, https://www.nytimes.com/1994/12/11/nyregion/cuttings-now-it-can-be-told-all-about-squirrels-and-nuts.html.

2. Abril McCloud, "Detour of the Year: How Burger King Swerved Its Way to 6MM Loyal App Users," *mParticle*, January 22, 2020, https://www.mparticle.com/customers/burger-king-whopper-detour.

3. Louise Grimmer and Martin Grimmer, "Dolly Parton Is a 'Great Unifier' in a Divided America. Here's Why," *The Conversation*, via ABC News, November 24, 2019, https://www.abc.net.au/news/2019-11-25/how-marketers-measure-dolly-partons-magic/11733972.

Index

Read more from Mike Michalowicz

- Free Resources and Tools for Your Marketing
- Join Our Workshops and Training Sessions
- Ensure you do *Get Different* right!

GoGetDifferent.com